WHAT, ON I
ARE WE DOING?

and
OTHER POEMS

AN ANTHOLOGY
by
LLOYD KEMP

ISBN: 978 – 1 – 905795 – 19 – 2
Published by Aspect Design
and printed and bound at their premises
89 Newtown Road, Malvern, WR14 1PD

CONTENTS

PREFACE

Until very recently (that is, the last five of my ninety-four years) writing a poem had been a spasmodic occurrence, and always by way of a response to significant events, either in my own life, or in the world at large.

It is not surprising, therefore, that the oldest surviving poem is 'God's Atoms', written in the early 1950s, and prompted by the development of the hydrogen bomb (to my great dismay) by my fellow physicists. *En passant,* it must be said that when, in 1932, I decided to read physics at University, it was the chemists who were in the business of dreaming up weapons of mass destruction, and I felt secure in my conviction that physics was, and would remain "pure" science, and was *inherently incapable* of being misused in such ways. How wrong can you be? – it was beyond imagining that, within a mere thirteen years, the first atom bomb would be exploded over a crowded city: hence the intensity of the feelings expressed in that particular poem.

Likewise, when, in 1968, my beloved wife Mary was struck down - totally unexpectedly - by the first of a series of severe strokes, this event and its aftermath produced, over the following twenty years and more, a whole series of poems documenting the courage, and total lack of self-concern, with which she faced the trials and tribulations which confronted her for the remainder of her life. Again, when my equally beloved younger son, Roger, collapsed and died one morning in February, 2005, the only way I could cope at all with this - and the sense of almost unimaginable loss that it involved - was to write about it in a series of poems, all composed within a few weeks of his tragic death. These poems, together with those written for Mary, appear together in a separate section, at the end of this Anthology.

Apart from a handful in classical sonnet form, and one or two others in strict metrical form (to create a special effect), the poems are in "free verse" form; and whilst metaphor, allegory, and – yes – symbolism are freely employed, it is always with the intent of clarifying meaning, rather than to make it more esoteric. Times are urgent, and – for my part, at any rate – call for communication of what is perceived as important to be direct and urgent, too.

Any attempt such as this to give some account of when and why I write poetry would fall seriously short of its objective if it failed to mention how another poem of mine, The Currency of Love', came into being. (From what I am told by friends and others with whom I have shared this particular poem, it is deemed by many to be the best poem I have written, or, for that matter, am ever likely to write!). For that reason you might be surprised to learn that its very *raison d'être* was the computerisation, in 1987, of the London Stock Exchange. So, 'What has love to do with the Stock Exchange?', you might well ask. Of course, the clue is in that word 'currency'. The fact is that I was so incensed by all the hullabaloo that went on at the time about the importance of money, and the ease with which it should be able to be exchanged (for the purpose of making more, of course), that I woke around 4 am a few mornings after the event, and wrote down this poem, almost as though it were being dictated. Perhaps it was! – a number of my poems concerning the deepest aspects of this human life of ours have 'arrived' in that way - unheralded by any forethought, and subject, subsequently, to little or no revision.

'The Currency of Love' deserves, I believe, its placement at the end of the group of poems written for Mary and Roger, both of whom loved so many, and so much.

The Anthology itself is divided into three groups of poems: 'In Lighter Vein', 'The Everyday', and 'The Spirit'. The first two groups are virtually self-explanatory, though I feel it worth commenting that they provide a necessary counterbalance to the third group: I would not want the latter to dominate the anthology. Yes, indeed – to nurture the life of the Spirit in ourselves and others is, I believe, what gives meaning and purpose to this human life of ours. Nevertheless, without a sense of humour, and the ability to "see the funny side of things", the work of the Spirit would be much more difficult, and, at times, bordering on the impossible. So! – I hope that you will enjoy my encounters with dandelions, spiders, night intruders, and the like, to say nothing of the poems scattered over all three groups, dealing with occasional contretemps with my computer!

Finally, I should point out that, within each section of the Anthology, the poems have been arranged *in alphabetical order of their titles.* This may seem a rather arbitrary, and even odd thing to do, but the alternative - of finding a *logical* basis for their ordering - defeated me. In fact. alphabetical ordering of the titles seemed a very good way of *randomising* the order, and, in places, this has produced quite interesting results!

And, in case the title of this Anthology should be thought to involve merely a mild exclamation, I would point out that the poem of which it is the title is very deeply concerned with the matter of climate change on this Earth of ours.

Lloyd Kemp, Bath, 2008

PROLOGUE

Light years, and chromosomes, and Saturn's rings
rub shoulders in my mind — or so it seems —
with shuttles, microchips, and laser beams:
familiar, yes, am I, with many things.

Familiar, too, with mountain's splashing springs,
sky's arching bow, and raindrops' smell on dust;
with wind's sough through high trees, and bread's crisp crust;
with lover's touch — and slaughter earthquake brings.

Yes, too familiar by far am I
with all life's haunting panoply of joy,
sharp sorrow, truth, half-truth, near-lie
that headlines economically employ.

Oh! whence shall come the power to lift the pall
familiarity has cast, o'er all?

IN LIGHTER VEIN

CONTENTS

------------A Good Smoke------------

'Take *that!* – and
put it in your pipe
and *smoke* it',
the words delivered
like a boxer's
knock-out punch.
But, 'Take *this!*' say I,
barely concealing
my excitement, 'and
no health warning on the
packet, either – its contents,
in fact, guaranteed
to *improve* your health,
even as you smoke it:
you *see* better,
you *hear* better,
and your heart
is enabled to
respond more fully
to the demands
life makes on it!'

'You'd like to try it
for yourself? That's fine! –
but there *is* one word
of warning, and it
doesn't come amiss:
it's strong stuff this,
and you may find –
at first acquaintance –
that you choke on it
a bit. But, take
my word for it,
it's well worth
persevering with;
and (note this, too)
the guarantee's for life.

'What's it called? Ah –
that's the other thing:
a single word (or even
two) wouldn't – couldn't
possibly suffice to convey
what it's all about.
So! Wait for it! –
you'd never have
guessed – it's called
*"Putting yourself in the
other chap's shoes."*

'You're not so sure
you want to try it now?
Go on! Stuff some
in that pipe of yours –
and put a match to it.
Go *on!* Have a go!
And you'll find
it won't just *glow* –
it'll light up the whole
neighbourhood, and more.

'You're *still* not sure?'

"Auntie"

She had been a favourite
with the family, her long life
through – from the oldest,
nearing twenty now, to the
youngest, barely two – that
neat little bonnet, from which
she just would not, *could* not
be separated, firmly placing her
in a previous generation, but
giving no clue as to what
lay hidden beneath it:
the strength, the character,
that had enabled her to get by
in so many tight corners –
when death itself
seemed near.

But, sadly, time takes its toll of
even the most stalwart, and she,
whom they had all known –
so affectionately – as "Auntie",
had been so suddenly taken
from their midst, each, in
his, or her own way, bidding
their last farewell, shedding
a quiet tear, as she began to
disappear round the bend
at the end of the road,
ignominiously being
towed, on her two
rear wheels, to the
breakers' yard.

Belated Birthday Card

At nearly ninety four
one's memory
(to say the least of it)
is bordering on the poor,
and when life gets
a little hectic
(as it has, for me, of late)
it's useless to expect it
to remember every
birthday, and
its date.
So! – do I
hear you say,
'I'll forgive you
just this once.'?

And fervently
I hope, too,
that my gift
(albeit modest)
will help you feel
less sad about, and
even a little
more glad about an
un-remembering Dad...

Betrayal

How can I tell you what I feel? –
you who had, for so long,
shared with me my darkest
moments, and my brightest
joys; who had faithfully taken them
to your heart, and stored them there,
like a good friend always does. And
in that prodigious memory of yours! –
a memory which, among those
who know you well, had earned
the reputation of being almost
limitless, ever willing and able
to recall the confidences I had
shared with you, however long ago;
you who had such incredible ability –
ability that you were always ready
to place at my disposal, and
at a moment's notice;
effortlessly, it seemed,
and never failing me.

   Or so it was – till now.
   Almost without warning then – and
   at a moment when my need of you
   was so great – you faltered:
   at first just a hesitation, and then
   something that amounted to
   plain reluctance to respond to
   my requests.

At first, I was unwilling to believe that
you were capable of such behaviour,
especially towards one who had always
treated you with such loving-kindness
and respect. But, alas, you persisted,
making it more than clear that
you had changed completely –
that your friendly collaboration,
for so long, and so productive,
was, most decisively,
at an end. Computer! –
you have *crashed*...

Confidences

Tonight, for the first time
that I had noticed,
my computer was
honouring me with a
touching little confidence:
'No input signal,' it said,
[so] 'I'm going to sleep.'

And (quite moved) I exclaimed,
'Well – *that* goes for *both* of us!'

But it made no reply:
it just went out like a light,
as likewise, shortly afterwards,
did I.

What *is* it about the number ten
that keeps grown men awake
at night? – the batsman who,
"on ninety-nine", was out next ball,
to fall "one short of his hundred";
grown women, too, who, happy
when they went to bed, wake,
next morning, in need of
an anti-depressant, having –
with no opt-out clause –
"turned forty", overnight.

And fifty follows far too fast,
when, on the stroke of midnight,
middle age sets in; followed
in no time at all (it seems)
by sixty – when women, in the
instant, metamorphose
to "senior citizens"
(though men take
half of ten years more,
before they're knocking
at the selfsame door).
And, looming ominously
not far ahead,
that venerated milestone
of "three score years and ten",
past which we're apt to feel
we live on borrowed time.

Yet do *some* benefits accrue
from this con-*ten*-tious
march of time: to wit,
for those who, half of
ten years further on,
are deemed worthy of
TV, for free. And, yes,
to offset the cold feet
that you may well get
when you've passed
the sixty mark, there's
the "winter fuel allowance"
of twenty times ten pounds.
(And should your age
reach *eight* times ten
you get another hundred;
maybe, by then, you've got
cold hands as well.)

There have been – and still are –
some notable exceptions
that serve only to prove the rule:
the erstwhile "golden guinea",
favoured unit of consultants' fees
and classic horse-race prizes
(its roots in snobbery – but
a subtle means of adding
five per cent to the fees,
without using bigger numbers...)
And, still alive, though
maybe no longer kicking,
the cult of the duodecimal,
based on the number twelve:
twelve inches to the foot,
with three times that number
to the yard; and eggs
still bought and sold
in multiples of six and twelve –
how otherwise could we assert
that things are "cheaper by the
dozen"?

But, there is just *one* exception,
which, far from proving the rule,
is constantly abusing it,
with the object? –
simply to mislead;
and the culprit? –
ten's un-neighbourly
next-door neighbour
nine, prepared to occupy
as many denary digits as it takes,
to avoid the extra one: hence
the bottle of spring water,
priced at ninety-nine pence,
or the bottle of vintage wine,
going for nine pounds ninety-
nine – not to mention the
packaged holiday, offered at
no less (or ought one to have said
"no more"?) than nine hundred,
nine and ninety pounds.

A trifle ironical – is it not ? –
that a cricketer should be
so fraught, when,
to all intents and purposes,
he'd achieved his goal
of that extra denary digit,
whilst we (though hoodwinked
into thinking otherwise) had,
to all intents and purposes,
spent it.

Dyelemmer

The spelling ov an Inglish werd
herd even mor than wunce,
cood sumtymes
(and purrhaps kwite offun)
mayke yoo feel a donce,
and seam two bee abserd.

Four instunce:
wot wood yoo doo,
az a meer newkumma
from a forrun shaw,
connfrunted with werds lyke
"bough", "slough" and "cough",
"half", "scarf", and "laugh"? –
not to menshun
a fish's "gill",
and milk measherd
bye the "gill".

Wood yoo – inn
an orful fit of peak –
speak werds that
foke chooz rarther
knot too here,
thro upp yor hands
and stamp the flor?
Or – maw lykeli –
giv upp orltwogethur?

Witch?

From the Comfort of my Armchair

I saw a tall ship,
hove to, to the leeward
of a jut of land, its sails,
some shredded, flapping –
clapping like tired hands,
against the mast;

   to the windward of the
   headland the gale lashing,
   waves splashing, forks of
   lightning flashing, thunder
   crashing – endlessly
   reverberating round
   the bay.

And, sometimes, as I
sit, myself hove to in my
armchair, contemplating
the end of a hard day
spent living – well,
that's how I
see me...

Glass Eyes – and Watery Ones

I'd forgotten to draw the curtains
(it was "bible-black" outside);
moreover, it had started to rain –
the first drops already clinging
to the windowpane.

  As raindrops go,
  you would have to say
  there weren't that many of them;
  but, considering the deep-dark night,
  how was it that I knew how few?
  Or – for that matter – how many?

It's all to do with *cats'* eyes.
No! Not real ones,
but the disembodied kind,
made of glass: you know –
the ones that glow in your
headlights, on a country road
at night.

  You see, a short way
  up the road from me
  was a street lamp – out of
  sight from where I sat – but,
  the light from it? Oh, no!

Captured by those watery drops
as they clung to the windowpane,
it lit them up – yes! – just like the
cats' eyes in the road – each one,
now, a brand-new, bright-yellow
star, set against the bible-black
where Orion might have been.

  And, with the empty sky, on that
  rainy night, so unexpectedly
  peopled by a bevy of bright stars
  new-born, I began, light-heartedly,
  to christen them, constellation
  upon constellation, with – oh –
  such fancy names!

That is, until the raindrops
started to join forces,
and, together – like
spent meteors – began
streaking down the glass.

  And the night –
  alas – became
  plain bible-black
  again.

Home Sounds from Abroad

I phoned a friend,
nine thousand miles away,
and – despite the miles –
he seemed to be
'just round the corner',
as they say.

But, when –
in his house –
a clock chimed the hour,
with other "noises off",
then he seemed to come
right round that corner, and
straight into the room
with me.

Life's Ups and Downs

It's true that those at the
bottom will strive to get
to the top, whilst there are
those who, having attained
such lofty status, find
it impossible to
continue to occupy
the dizzy heights, and
slowly, inexorably, sink
to the bottom again.

It's also true that
those who, having opted
to be bystanders, yet find a
certain voyeuristic fascination
in watching the lowly climb, and
an even greater fascination
in witnessing the down fall
of those who, having reached
the top, discover their inability
to remain – the endless cycle
of ups and downs as public as
if it were taking place in the
proverbial goldfish bowl;

which, in truth, and
to all intents and purposes,
it was – bathed in the
yellow light of my
Lava Lamp.

Lost Bearings

It could have been a dream –
or even a nightmare:
on a brief holiday, I found myself
high up, and alone in the dark –
surrounded on almost every side
by a vertical drop.

   I lay flat on my stomach,
   fearful of going over the edge,
   my feet from time to time
   left dangling in empty space.

I struggled for a light,
to reassure myself that
I was near the middle, and
not too close to the edge of
what was so strange to me now
(and far too big):

a double bed.

Lost It?

I dropped a pound coin
as I boarded the bus, and
before I could even
begin my awkward
"stoop and bend" routine
a young lad – yet to reach
his teens – had jumped to
his feet, and immediately
retrieved it. 'No prob!'
he exclaimed expansively,
as I endeavoured to
express my thanks.

  'Did you know,' I volunteered,
  'that the floor gets further
  and further away, the
  older you become?'

But my attempt at
humour failed
dismally
to bridge the
generation gap:
he simply smiled
indulgently at
someone who was
plainly in his
dotage.

Miscarriage of Justice — or Was It?

It was, without doubt, an
extreme example of the
invasion of one's privacy;
my door often "on the latch" —
and sometimes slightly ajar —
but I'm sure he'd obtained
entry surreptitiously, in
some quite other
way.

But, even when
I first caught sight
of him, his condition
was bordering on the
moribund, and I resented
the circumstances that
would inevitably lead to
my opting for the line of
least resistance; in short,
to resort to justice that was —
yes — summary.

Yet, would *you* have
done otherwise, had you —
like me — found, just *after*
getting in, that you were
sharing your bath with
an outsize specimen
of the *arachnida?*

There was, indeed,
nothing else for it:
it *had* to be "*death
by drowning*".

My Waterloo!

I saw my face
reflected
by the water
in the loo;
it was a funny place
to see oneself,
and I wondered
what to do –
so I put the lid down
firmly, and hastily
withdrew.

----------- **Night Intruder** -----------

I woke, fearful,
as from a nightmare;
but the fear was still there
as I lay, wide-eyed, knowing –
somehow – that I'd
not simply *awakened,* but
had been *woken up* – by
something, or even
somebody.

There it was!
A sound! – and,
horror of horrors,
it could well have been
the squeak of a very large rat.

I lay, petrified, as I pondered what
loathsome creature had invaded my
house and home – and how? – perhaps
when I took the rubbish out
to the bin, last thing, and
left the door wide open?

Gingerly,
I got out of bed,
and lowered my feet
to the floor. A few strides, and
I'd slammed the bedroom door.
There it was again! – but weaker now:
whatever it was, at least, thanks be,
it was outside, in the hall.

I eased the door open and listened –
and there it was, yet again. But
this time I realized that it
could just as well be
the squawk of a
very large bird.

A bundle of nerves, I took just
one stride, out into the hall,
and stood, stock still –
and I hadn't long to wait:
once more, the sound,
and this time *directly*
over my head.

Somehow, then,
I forced myself to look up,
my imagination working overtime
on what fearsome surprise might
greet my half-averted eyes.

And there it was –
stuck on the ceiling –
and emitting its warning call,
which meant no more, no less,
than "Low Battery" in
the Smoke Alarm.

Nightlights

Awakening,
in the small hours,
to quench my thirst –
and there, through a
chink in the curtains,
is that light again.
Yes – whatever
the time, whichever
the night, it's there;
to me not just
a light in a window
that might equally well
be dark, but having a
tale to tell – could I but
read it right:

is he an owl, who thinks
nothing of going to bed
when the rest of the world
is waking up? – or, worse,
an insomniac, having to
bear his own company
at such time of night;
or, worse still, afraid
of the darkness,
without, within,
and the spectres
lurking there.

But wait! –
my window's
lighted, too! – so
what will he make
of that, should he see?
Will he be thinking the
same of me? Or will he
just feel grateful that –
though but briefly –
he's now got
company?

November

It was first light – meditation time –
and I looked up from my book
to say 'Good Morning' to the world:
to the sky, bright enough now
to put the stars to bed;
to the distant hills and their
skyline, the fields below, and the
rooftops in the valley, and even to
that invasive phone pole,
upstaging everything
in view. But all I saw
was mist on
glass.

    Could the inner warmth
    of faith, I wondered,
    overcome the cold
    of doubt without, and
    clarify my view
    of the world?

(My meditation
had resumed!)

Of Prime Importance

It's all three:
adjective, noun, and verb;
but, when adverbs
were being handed out,
passed over, inexplicably.

   Let's not be greedy, though:
   as *adjective* alone there are
   "prime" concerns, "prime" cuts
   of meat, and "prime" examples, too –
   to say nothing of "prime" numbers
   (beloved of the mathematician),
   the "prime" cost of a commodity, and
   "prime" rate, too (as charged by banks);
   nor must we overlook the "prime"
   meridian, that bestows on
   Greenwich a singular
   distinction, as it
   passes through.

And – Heaven for*bid!* –
let's not forget "prime" minister,
hopefully, still, in the "prime" of life,
and regularly given "prime" time
on the box, as a "prime" mover
in all manner of radical reforms,
for which there is, undeniably,
a "prime" need

   And the *verb?* –
   much less in evidence, we must agree,
   but nonetheless, we acknowledge,
   thankfully, the services of those who,
   daily, "prime" for action our engines
   and our pumps – or indeed simply
   "prime" (with a coat of paint).

More serious, though, is "prime"
as *noun:* the first of eight positions
adopted by a fencer prior to
launching a parry (or even
an attack); and "Prime" – quite
solemn this – the second of
seven services, that make up
the Divine Office

   But, last, and, most solemn of all,
   is – among philosophical terms–
   "the Prime Mover", graced
   by capital letters, and
   signifying none less than
   Almighty God.

------------On the Bus------------

A poem was brewing
as I clambered aboard,
eager to reach a seat,
where I could resort
to the time-honoured
back of an envelope,
before my short-term
memory had finally
deserted me, and I
was left, stranded,
with nothing to show
for my excitement:
an angler, dangling
an empty hook.

The ticket machine
jammed, and the driver,
venting his spleen on me,
demanded to see my pass –
as if my white hair (that is,
what little is left of it)
was not evidence enough
that I (and my incipient
poem) was entitled to
half-fare. I fumbled, and
found the pass, impatiently
waving it in his face, my
eyes already on
an empty place.

At last I was seated,
and, disposing of my stick,
I sought that all-important
envelope. A pen, then, and
eagerly I began to write –
short lines, as is my wont –
unaware that I was
being watched.

Vacantly,
I looked up
as I pondered,
and caught the eye
of the lady sitting opposite,
who had fixed me with a stare.

'Doing your shopping list?'
she asked (she was one of
the chatty kind), 'It's so easy –
isn't it, dear? – I mean –
to forget what it was
you had in mind.'

'It is! It is!' I said – with a
fervour for shopping lists
that I could hardly have
expected her to
understand.

Over-exposure?

It must have been
his umpteenth-plus-one
attempt at recording her
for posterity, and she was
doing her best to smile in a
way she hadn't done on the
umpteen times before. But –
let's face it – she was
finding it difficult, and
had ended up with a
somewhat silly simper:
not surprising really,
after umpteen attempts
to look as though it was
for the first time ever.

She was standing before
the West Door of the
Abbey – massive,
of solid oak, and
carved in bas-relief;
and I wondered –
was the photograph
intended to be of
her, the *door,* or (two for
the price of one)
of *both?*

Competing previously
(may be) with backdrops
like the Arc de Triomphe,
the Statue of Liberty,
and (who knows?) even
the Taj Mahal, it may
have been nothing new
to her: attempting to
outshine a solid oak
West Door.

But perhaps, in his
adoring eyes, it
wasn't like that
at all – *they* were
competing
with *her*...

Peek-a-boo!

The bus was jam-packed,
all seats occupied, and bodies
standing, shoulder to shoulder,
the length of the gangway:
a human wall, dividing
the bus, one side
from the other –
apart from the chinks
below abutting shoulders,
and the gaps in the
palisade of legs.

My apprehension grew. What if
the bus stopped suddenly? – and
what chance, at my destination,
of reaching the door in time?
Worse still, the ventilation:
what had lately been a bus
fast becoming a veritable
Black Hole of Calcutta.

Claustrophobia, slowly but surely,
was getting its grip on me, as eyes,
with nothing else to occupy them,
dropped towards the floor and
those gaps in that palisade of
legs – as if, somehow, they
might provide a route for
my escape.

But, it seemed that apprehension, in an
unholy union with claustrophobia,
had given birth to hallucination.
For there, in one of the gaps,
appeared what could have been
the face of an angel: my Guardian,
perhaps? – and come to
rescue me?

But further inspection
revealed it to be, in
truth, the face of a little
girl, inviting me to
play "Peek-a-boo",
between the
pairs of legs.

An angel?
Maybe not (and she
all but made me
miss my stop) –

but, nevertheless,
a god-sent cure
for claustrophobia.

Permission to Use Expletives

'My God!' he might have
exclaimed (that is, if he had one).
'Struth!' he might well have
added, as he looked about him –
'Blime!' had he been given to
blaspheming, and *'You could have
knocked me down with a feather!'*
if of more humorous disposition.

Who, for Pete's sake,
could it have been,
and what had he seen? –
a Martian, brought up
on dull brick-red, on a
maiden mission
to our Planet?

Or –
what price simply
a member of the
human race, eyes
opening, as it were,
for first time ever
on Mother Earth?

Phoney Feelings

I dialled the number
in keen anticipation –
eager to exchange
news and views
with a friend.

  A short delay, and
  the phone was ringing,
  summoning him
  to a chat.

Again,
and yet again,
it rang, as my
disappointment grew,
until, suddenly –
inanimate object though
it was – I began to feel a
strange sense akin to
pity for it, as I became
aware of the forlornness
of its task, continuing, as it
did, to issue its stillborn
summons to an empty
house – and to
someone who
wasn't there.

Pickpocket

A well-loved, well-worn
jacket, retrieved from the
dim recesses of a
wardrobe, or an
anorak, rediscovered
in the autumn, in
response to a
freshening wind –
each can be like a
special edition of
"Lloyd Kemp –
This is Your Life":

   in the pockets an
   "all-day" bus ticket,
   six months out-of-date,
   and a till receipt
   which showed that, on the
   ninth of February last,
   I had purchased from
   Marks and Spencer
   six bananas, two
   "Little Gem" lettuce,
   and a single, large
   red onion;

a screwed-up leaflet, too,
suggesting that I'd chosen
quite the wrong company
when I'd re-insured my house,
and pointing out how quickly
I could put the matter right.
Two handkerchiefs, then, and
a third in another pocket
(so *that's* why I thought
I was getting short).
And – *Hey!* What's *this?* – a
pound coin, hiding in the
fluff! – Oh, *boy!* – am I
in clover! And,
what *next?* Ah –

that letter I
insisted had
got lost in
the post.

Pressing Matters

'All I had to do,' he said,
'was to press the button
twice!' He spoke as if he were
sharing one of the darker
secrets of the Universe –
which, in a way, he was:
his latest acquisition
a box of technological
wizardry which should have
played his DVDs, but was
playing up, instead.
And the trick? –
yes! – was simply to
press a single button
not once, but twice,
and – hey presto! –
all was well.

   A generation
   of button pressers, we
   expect – and get – miracles
   performed by our button-
   pressing proclivities: press
   but a few, and money comes
   tumbling from a hole in a
   wall; a few more, and you're
   talking to someone as far away
   as Singapore. Press a button
   on your microwave, and you can
   cook a meal with (so it seems)
   no heat at all... And what about
   walking, whilst talking on your
   mobile? – to say nothing of
   that single button pressed to
   wash the dirty dishes, or
   all your grubby clothes; to
   change the TV programme
   from the comfort of your chair,
   boot up your computer, toast
   bread, and even
   make – and bake – it.

It's all about
quality of life (they say).
And – yes – it's true, there's
often much to be gained
by pressing a button once
(or even twice); though
sometimes – just
*some*times – there's
much to be lost
as well.

(I simply *loved*
kneading the dough.)

Problem Solved

If it happens that life
is not all that it has been –
if you're finding it difficult
to perform the simplest of
tasks, and, even if you
pull yourself together
and manage to respond,
it still takes aeons of time;
if, worse still, you
do the equivalent
of collapsing into an
armchair and closing
your eyes and trying to
forget the world in
sleep: if all this
should be the case –
then, take heart! All is
far from lost. Just peep
into your diary (so to say)
and find a day when
you made a note that
this would be one of those
that you would like to
return to, and, hey presto! –
in next to no time – all is
well: life can begin again;
and those seemingly
insurmountable
obstacles, that had
made it too difficult to
bear, simply not there
any more.

That is, if you're a
computer, with
"System Restore"
installed.

----------- Public Puddle -----------

One would not expect a puddle
to acquire its own identity –
but the one I came to know so well
had acquired, not merely an identity
but a local habitation, and
(all but) a name.

Far removed
from the anonymity of
a country lane, it put in
a public appearance
after every shower of rain –
to demonstrate, in breadth
and depth, a character rarely
encountered on the prestigious
pavements of a city the likes
of Georgian Bath.

Indeed, truth is that
it owed its very existence
to a (metaphorical) handful of
paving slabs, whose inexplicable
subsidence had long since passed
into the history of a back street
that was otherwise undeserving
of any special note.

But – came the day when all was
no longer as it should be with
the water, gas, or electricity
(it matters not which): up came
the slabs, and there began a
surgical procedure, feet
below ground. Whether for
hydraulic hernia, electrical
excesses, or gaseous goings-on,
the operation on Mother
Earth was tedious, and long.
Eventually, though, the job was
done, the patient cured – and the
wound sealed over with those
erstwhile out-of-kilter slabs.

Never again would I linger by the
urban pool, to contemplate the
rows of chimney pots apparently
below ground, or people walking
upside down in the sky – to say
nothing of a devil-may-care
return to childhood, and the
delight of wading through a
puddle deep enough to
challenge shoes.

But the sense of loss became
astonishment when I found
(believe it as you may, or not)
that the workmen – displaying
rare initiative – had, in fact,
restored, not only Mother Earth,
but – yes, you've guessed! –

the puddle, too.

Refreshment Time

Sometimes it's a case
of being overburdened
by the past, or an inability
to deal with the present, or –
worse still – a refusal to accept
what the future is demanding.

   No! – it's not me – it's my
   computer screen, and it needs
   "refreshing" (that's Microsoft-
   Speak for it).

☐uite simply, by left-clicking
on a single button, one is able –
yes! – to "refresh" it, and
all is well again: with past
put firmly behind it,
the future no longer
a paralysing threat,
the screen is once more
able to accept what
life demands of it.

(Could we but be
thus easily
"refreshed"!)

Retirement

Their lives had been long and
active, participating, as they had,
in the whole gamut of human affairs,
from the most auspicious of
public occasions to the humble
circumstances of family
hearth and home.

But, despite their
sterling qualities, they had
reached the time when life had
begun to pass them by – no longer
participants in the big events, or the
"trend setters" that, in their heyday,
they had been; yet was this the
very moment when those sterling
qualities of theirs had again
come into play:

two forks, each prong
bent in a different 'come-hither'
gesture, and two spoons, bowls
beaten flat, and all four
suspended from hooks that
kept them well apart: that is,
until they were blown together –
chiming – in the wind.

Would that I could make as
pleasing sounds as they, when –
in *my* retirement – the
wind is blowing hard.

Small Mercies –
Yet the Blessings Big

Lord,
I thank you
that my foot
is barely swollen, and
doesn't hurt me very much;
that, when I walk,
hardly ever does it
impede even a single
step, far less threaten to
bring me to a halt.
So it is that I offer up
my inward-bound
big-toenail, that it may
continue, faithfully
to refrain from
hampering your plans
for me, for this –
a whole new
day.

Snapshot

Perched high on
a chimney pot,
stock-still, and
silhouetted against
a bright-white cloud,
was a blackbird – looking
more like a weathercock,
bone idle on a
windless day.

Special Delivery

"Berliner Pott" was the inscription
on its side: "Berlin Mug" – but neither
"Pott" nor "Mug" doing justice to its
elegant appearance, or the place
it has won in the daily round of
my domestic life.

    Blue the wording, and
    "*out* of the blue" it had arrived –
    unexpected and unannounced –
    complete with German-grown black tea,
    "sehr kräftige, und stark aromatish".

And, as if *that* weren't enough,
there were little wooden sticks,
like miniature stone-age cudgels,
one end weighted with a solid clump
of sugar with which to stir your
"cuppa" and, simultaneously,
sweeten it.

    Direct from Berlin it had come –
    "Special Delivery", it had seemed
    to me. And the young lady who'd
    sent it? Well! – she just *had* to be
    special, too!

A pleasant surprise! - following a visit from Jeremy, my German grandson,
and his girl-friend Edna.

Special Offers

At ninety-one,
I could hardly claim to
be a computer buff,
but nevertheless I
make good use of one.
And, today, I received an offer
that I'm finding hard to ignore:
a one-off payment of just seventy
pounds, entitling me, for the next
three years (if things go wrong),
to unlimited visits from a computer
practitioner, with free, and immediate
replacement of any hardware
found to have broken down.

What an offer! –
and it set me wondering:
what if I were to receive a similar one
from my *medical* practitioner? – of
as many visits from such specialists
as are deemed necessary, with
free, and immediate, replacement
of any defective parts.

What more could I ask,
when I'm ninety-four?

Surprise! Surprise!

My computers has a logic
all its own. Thus, to stop it
you must first press "START", and
only then are you offered
the choice to "LOG OFF" – or
"TURN OFF" altogether.

   And, whilst the choice to
   "TURN OFF" might be thought to
   be the end of it, it's far from so:
   you are promptly presented with
   the tempting alternatives to
   "STAND BY", or – guess what! –
   (but, no! – you never will) to –
   yes! – *"RESTART"* it…

And then – to make sure
you know what you've done
(and with triumphal tones
accompanying) – it quietly
informs you that it really *is*
"LOGGING OFF"– and that it's
"SAVING YOUR SETTINGS", too
(surely an eleventh-hour
conversion to the cause?).

   And, finally, the screen
   (and one could well imagine it
   flushing pink with pride)
   portentously informs you
   that "WINDOWS (and question it
   no more!) ***IS*** SHUTTING DOWN" –
   to which the only
   adequate response
   just *has* to be
   "AMEN".

(But –
sad to say –
Bill Gates has
yet to think of that.)

Survival

In my time,
how I've disliked you! – even
detested you – for what you are:
seemingly a total misfit, so that
many would have it that there is
no place for you in this world –
that it might have been better
had you never existed.

But – we have to face it –
you are here, and, with the
rest of us, you breathe God's air,
though opinion has it that
every effort should be made to
make life as difficult as possible,
should you attempt to take up
residence among a cultured,
and thriving population
of your kith and kin.

Yet have I to admit that when
I came upon one of your number
but a day or so ago, you were not
in fact trying to elbow your way
into company where you would
indeed have been unwelcome –
rather, were you displaying
an ability to live
in circumstances in which the
vast majority of your kind
would have found it impossible
even to set up home,
let alone survive.

Would that I had your capacity,
not only to survive, but even to
thrive, in conditions as harsh as
those you were facing where I
found you – roughing it, all alone,
in a mere crevice,
in a tarmac-ed
pavement!

Oh, *dandelion!* –
teach me
how.

The Agony of Doubt

He fell to his knees,
and his arms shot skyward,
spread wide, as if to embrace
the length, breadth, and height
of the overarching sky – his eyes
pleading, as with the Deity,
for release from the awful
uncertainty into which events
had so suddenly
plunged him.

Others gathered round,
sharing the doubt that
had overtaken him, and
echoing that one word he had
involuntarily screamed –
for, and on behalf of
the countless thousands who,
looking on, understood,
all too well, his agony of mind –
'Owzat!'

But the umpire
(who, for the occasion,
was standing in for God)
solemnly shook his head.

The Alexander Technique

Between the act
and its prompting thought
there is a moment, which –
going unobserved –
condemns the act to
mere impulse,
born of instinct,
and fathered by no-one:
a waif among waifs,
peopling the
undirected hours.

But,
mark that moment with a
pause, charged with paying
due regard to means whereby
the act, crucially delayed,
shall be given true parentage
in conscious thought –
comprise a choice from
options kept open till the
instant of their resolution –
mark the moment thus,
and body-mind shall act
in concert: an entity,
no longer driven before
instinct's gusty blow,
but held in balance
by the "means-whereby",
in that crucial, moment's
pause.

And the "means-whereby"?
Ah! – what can stem
from lengthened,
widened back,
neck loose, head
forward,
up!

The Worm and the Walking Stick

Perambulating along
an unforgiving pavement
with my trusty walking stick,
accidentally I all but planted it
on an earthworm far from home.

Pausing for a moment
to pay my respects to
a fragment of Life that could
so easily have been no more,
I walked on, and, as I went,
I pondered the fact that
my stalwart aid to easier
movement had come so near
to terminating movement
altogether, for a helpless
fellow creature.

But, then, a further thought:
stranded, as it was, on a
tarmac desert, a day's wriggle
from the paradise of a
well-kept compost heap,
would I, in fact, have been
doing the poor critter a
good turn, had I, indeed, put
an end to it – albeit accidentally –
whilst out walking,
with my stick?

Time and Motion Study

The symphony orchestra –
full hundred strong – and
a choir of equal number,
had just performed the
Beethoven Ninth. And,
suddenly, I found myself
day-dreaming:

   in the audience a *very* excited
   man, an entrepreneur, wondering
   what a work force of two hundred plus
   could have produced in the sixty-
   two minutes and nineteen seconds
   of the performance, had they been
   more profitably engaged than
   producing mere sound waves
   that were no sooner here than gone.
   What productivity! What profitability!
   'Gee! what couldn't I do with a work force
   like that, pulling together, as one!'

He went up, and stood by the conductor.
'Say, guys! – *and* dolls! – come and work
for me! I'll double your salary on the spot!
Oh! boy! how I want what you have got!'

   But he was confused –
   not to say dismayed –
   when, to a guy (and a doll),
   they turned his offer down.
   'I don't know what the world
   is *coming* to,' he was
   heard to mutter,
   disconsolately.

Time-Out

I used to think
that time warps
were the sole
prerogative
of the writers of
sci-fi. But, no longer:
with my very eyes
I witnessed a
living example –
and only the
other day.

Two people there were,
who, having reached
the moment of decision,
had opted out of time
as we know it, and
succeeded in slowing
its passing at least
tenfold.

Nor had they
any regrets concerning
the choice they'd made –
able, still, to look
about them, at the
life they'd left behind,
and – with almost
childlike innocence –
rejoicing in their choice,
as the old life continued
to swirl past them,
frenetically as ever,
and they drank in
the experiencc
of re-living the life
of Regency Bath
in a horse-drawn
cabriolet.

Twosome

It takes two to
tango (so they say),
and, yes – it's true –
there *were* two,
but no tango were
they dancing, as they
flitted to and fro:

anything but slinky,
their movements
fast but by no means
furious, and with eyes for
nothing but each other
(and objects to avoid),
endlessly gyrating, in
seeming ecstasy –
celebrating together,
a sunny afternoon:
two cabbage whites.

We need to Rise Twice – (Like Bread!)

Yes! I'm up!
But rising
from my bed
is not enough:
we need to rise
to the occasion –
and that's
not nearly as easy
as getting out of bed.

Willing Accomplice

It used to be the clatter of
type-bars on platens of rubber –
or a pen pursuing its convoluted
course across sheets of man-made
paper; and, earlier still, a feathered
quill scratching its way across the
surface of dried goat's skin (no
fountain concealed within its
hollow shaft: quenching its thirst,
as needed, at a shallow well,
of ink).

Gone now the type-bars' clatter,
no longer pen on paper, or quill
on parchment sheet: just the
LCD of my computer, and the
cursor, blinking impatiently:
horse champing at the bit;

and – like me – ready, and
rearing to go!

THE EVERYDAY

CONTENTS

A Passing Lorry

They had seemed undeserving
of a second glance, as the lorry,
grossly overburdened by them,
struggled past, protesting as it went.
After all, what could be less worthy
of note than three huge hunks
of rough-hewn stone?

But, as the lorry lumbered on,
I looked again, and no longer
did I see the three blocks as they
were, but as they would be, when
the sculptor's hammer and chisel
had done their work, and revealed
the secrets, long dormant, within
their drab exterior.

And the lorry? Ah − I saw that
as enjoying a very privileged
old age.

----------- **A Tale of Two Dogs** -----------

That first dog – it was very large,
even for a retriever; not only was it
on a lead, but muzzled, too,
a narrow leather thong tight,
round its jaws, but it didn't seem
to worry: it had other things to do.

It was walking alongside its mistress –
neither straining at the lead, nor
hanging back; and as it walked,
it turned its head majestically
from side to side, for all the world
like a high dignitary, acknowledging
the cheering crowds: its demeanour
that of someone with a proud mission
to discharge – nothing less, it seemed,
than portraying to the world at large
the quintessence of
what it means
to be a dog.

Stark indeed the contrast
with the other representative
of the canine species observed
but one day later: a "Jack Russell",
short-legged, long-bodied, highly-strung
and *bristling* with anxiety as it went,
eyes for nothing save its master;
its head cocked up and backward,
desperate to catch the slightest change
in facial expression that might portend
a new command to be answered
there and then, a new wish
to be fulfilled.

It hadn't even half an eye on whither
it went – all attention on its master;
and I fell to wondering whether the
Jack Russell had the edge on the
retriever in portraying
quintessential
dogginess – or
was it, maybe,
guilty of
excess?

------------A Taxing Driver------------

With the "diminishments"
that come with age,
my acquaintanceship
with taxi drivers has
inevitably grown –
a process much aided
by the practice of
travelling "in the front",
my intention, not only
to be chummy, but to
avoid, like the plague,
putting distance
between myself and
a fellow human being.

So was it that, on the first
of two memorable occasions,
I was seated beside the driver,
a young black man – and a
very friendly one, at that.
Predictably, we started with
the weather – was it going to rain?
Well – no – we hoped not, but
who could tell? – especially
in a country such as ours.

With the opening gambit over,
we moved on to other things –
the state of the roads, pollution,
the untrustworthiness of
politicians, and the
obscenities of war.
Indeed, so animated
had the conversation been,
that, after I'd dismounted, he
queried the time of my return,
keen – as he so obviously was –
for us to talk again. 'Sorry,' I said,
'that's something I don't even know
myself' – his disappointment plain.

Then, with but a day between,
I had need of another taxi,
and was waiting, expectantly,
on the pavement by my house.
It came – this time the driver
middle-aged, and white.

But, on his ears,
headphones clamped tight,
(his Walkman by his side) –
and, as if that weren't enough,
he was puffing at a pipe.

So – with his message
all to plain – I travelled
in the back.

After-Thoughts

Rose-red,
sharp-flavoured,
face downward on a plate
it lay – just half an apple,
the knife that you had used
to divide it, beside it, still:

    one half for you,
    the other half
    (it seemed just then)
    left, specially for me,
    its very presence so
    strangely redolent
    of you.

Wistfully,
I wondered: had not
my half, in the eating,
a sacramental role to play –
marking the bitter-sweetness
of your stay, all too brief, and
now so sudden
ended?

Written on arriving back home, after seeing off my daughter Rosemary
to her home in Germany, after a three-week stay.

An Unexpected Lift
(for Body *and* Spirit)

Of an age
when waiting at a
bus stop on a hot and
windy day is *not* –
to say the least of it –
my first choice of occupation,
I was whiling away the time
by counting the cars with three
spare seats, as they whizzed by,
and imagining myself
happily ensconced
in one of them.

Wishful thinking – yes –
but, on this particular day
there was more to come –
and, no, not just wishful
thinking, either: for I
fell to pondering
when (if ever) one such
had stopped, with the offer
of a lift. And,
believe it or not,
the very next one to
come along – *yes, the
very next one!* – hove to,
the driver young, his
accent unmistakably
foreign: 'You go my way?
I give you lift?'

Times are, when
we (quite rightly) say,
'I just could *not* believe
my ears.' And, climbing in,
I told him why I'd looked –
no – not just *surprised* but,
as he must have thought,
positively *astonished.*
 'Not so,' he said, 'You see –
perhaps it was to be.
These things happen,' he
added, almost casually.

And, in that moment,
it was as if a
third seat of the car
had been occupied by
One well known for
answering prayers in
unusual ways at
unusual times, and in
unexpected places.

At The Kitchen Sink

I was washing up, and
thinking, 'What a bore!' –
when suddenly it came
to me that at that moment
there were countless others,
not *washing* up, but being
beaten up, by so-called
fellow humans.

And – no more – would
the washing up
seem chore.

Autumn

The sun – hidden,
hitherto, behind a veil
of drab-grey cloud –
relented, peering out, on
a murky, mist-clad scene.

The mist, too, relented then,
and – choosing just one
from sunlight's seven-hued
dresses – bedecked itself
in lucent blue, to outshine
the beauty even of the
erstwhile-hidden view.

Big Brother

We sat, enjoying
our cups of tea —
the blue sky above, and
below, the quiet lap
of the sea.

Off-shore, the boats
were sailing slowly past,
propelled by a gentle
breeze, whilst lovers
walked hand-in-hand
along the promenade, and
children played on the sand,
or went swimming in the sea.
Could any*one,* or any*thing,*
question the peacefulness
of such a scene?

It seemed so:
hard by, a mast,
aiming for the sky,
but, atop which,
no festive flag.
Instead —
and peering,
aggressively,
up,
down,
round and about
and back again,
at cups of tea
and sailing boats,
lovers, and
children in the sea —

yes —
a CCTV camera,
desperate to
justify its
raison d'être by
looking for trouble
at a postcode
next to Heaven.

Blessing in Disguise

Ever the pride of
my gardening life, the
lawn had always received
Spring feeds (laced with
Death for Weeds) – and
followed by regular
autumn dressings, to
see the winter through.
Mowings twice a week
ensured fine growth, and
made doubly sure that
weeds had never a chance:
and the result? – a carpet of
living green, and a feast
for any gardener's eyes.

But, came the day
when old age, looming,
had taken its toll of
gardening muscle and
limb, and a patch of
the dreaded weeds
appeared, white and blue
speedwell, harbingers
of Spring;

and my heart
was cheered.

Bullowall Barrow, Cornwall

The blue-black sea, fringed green, and foaming white,
beleaguers rocky bastions below,
and spends itself in ceaseless ebb and flow,
as though performing some primeval rite.

Above, the gulls indulge their wheeling flight,
to add their own archaic sounds to sea's
slow slop on stubborn Cornish rock, and tease
the mind with ancient, half-recalled delight.

We stood beside the tri-millennial mound –
mere infant set midst nature's timeless dance –
and marvelled that men's hands alone built, bound
these massive stones, to stand thus long, perchance.
But, tri-millennium hence, may aught be found
of atom's age – or man, to cast a glance?

----------- Business NOT as Usual -----------

Charing Cross was
as busy as ever:
rumbling escalators
discharging their
human cargo into
the corridors below;
bewildered travellers
gazing hopefully
at direction signs –
jostled by those, who,
about their daily business,
would have known their way
blindfold.

Girls, stiletto-heeled,
bedecked in latest fashions,
ostentatiously displayed
their boredom, as they
waited for their train –
whilst young men, bowler-
hatted, and with all the other
trappings of their City uniform
(the rolled umbrella, and
handkerchief peeping
from breast pocket, or
draped carefully from sleeve –
white collared, old school tie),
scanned the columns of the
Financial Times, hoping
to discover how money
might be made quicker and
easier today, than yesterday.

Opposite the platform,
on the tunnel wall,
posters clamoured
to catch the eye,
declaring, variously,
that beer is best, milk
should be drunk daily –
and that Fruit Salts
had a beneficial effect
on the intestinal tract;
whilst, for the over-forties,
life could begin again
for a mere three shillings
(or was it five?)
a bottle.

Over this hurly-burly –
this meaningless medley
of things and people –
and above the rattle
of approaching trains,
there came the sound
of a man, whistling
unobtrusively –
like a blackbird singing
on a gable's end at
sundown – simply for
the joy of it.

And, in that moment, boredom
vanished from the powder-
daubed and painted faces
of the girls; the young men
lost interest in the closing prices
of gilt-edged shares – and
even the medicinal value
of Fruit Salts palled,
as a black man, a porter –
shut away from the sunshine
that, as a boy, he'd known so well –
whistled a chorus he'd learnt
at his mother's knee.

Slowly, down the dim corridors of
time, the words came back to me:
'Yes, Jesus loves me,
the Bible tells me so.'

☐uietly, lovingly, he lingered
on a tune whose words were
too simple for sophisticated ears,
until (who knows?) his song,
wordless albeit, broke through
the bowler-hatted barriers of the
City gents, and touched the
tight-lipped, boredom-feigning
girls, to reach their hearts,
as mine – in that moment,
a hundred feet below
the pavement of a
London street.

(1950s)

Cape Cornwall

The bluebells clothe the cliffs in deep-hued drifts,
amidst them, set like gems, the golden gorse.
Across the stream a cuckoo marks its course
with limpid call, to match Spring's choicest gifts.
Below, gulls squawk and squabble in the rifts
of rocks, as men prepare their puny boats
for sea; and lurid sun, near setting, floats,
serene above the Cape. The grey mist lifts;
and headland, black as jet 'gainst glittering sea,
defies the fading light of dying day,
inviting laggard traveller to be
its last late-lingering guest – in silence stay
the tide of anxious thought; then, spirit free
to greet the kindly night, be on his way.

(Ch)airborne

For what it cost
it might have been
her next-to-best
throne. After all —
to me — just then,
she *was* a queen:
queen of the
morning which,
at that hour, she
was sharing with
me alone, I
at my sink,
making an
early morning
cup of tea; and
she? You might say
that she was just
a passer-by — out
exercising
her dog.

    It's true — she was —
but you could
be forgiven for
thinking that,
in fact, the dog
was exercising
her: yards ahead, his
lead attached to the
(electrically-driven)
chair, which he firmly
believed he was
pulling.
        And sailing by,
she caught my eye,
waved 'Welcome to my
morning,' and bestowed
on me the priceless
favour of her smile,
which said — plainer than
any words — 'Yes, you're
right, I've got MS,
but it's still "top o' the
morning", for him
and me.'

(And —
then on —
for me, as well.)

Database

To a computer
they were mere data –
on a par with facts and
figures, and even formulae –
but, to me, they were
nothing less than the
names and addresses of
the intended recipients of
this year's Christmas cards.

  A double-click,
  and there they were! –
  all hundred and seven,
  in alphabetical order:
  family, friends, and
  acquaintances – in fact,
  an "A to Z" of my life;
  old friends, evoking
  a host of memories,
  a handful, new, their
  memories few; and one –
  just one – who had
  turned out to be
  no friend at all:
  my "A to Z", sadly,
  badly in need of
  editing.

Yet, did I take heart! –
with a database, it's
literally as simple as
ABC: for friends –
recently acquired –
just type them in,
and click on "Add";
(or – for the one
who'd failed me –
highlight, and then
just click "Remove").

  But what of those who,
  since last Christmastide, had,
  (as it is said) "passed on"? –
  computers just don't cater for
  such a turn of phrase.

In one way
it couldn't be easier:
just highlight the name,
and press "Remove" again.
But – not nearly so easy
to fill the gap it leaves
in the "A to Z" of life:
not even Bill Gates
offers software
to do that.

Deciding Moments
A Poem for the New Year

Doors offer choices:
between the inside
and the outside,
the familiar
and the unknown,
the warmth within
and the cold without –
the light, and
the darkness
of the night.

Choosing
is like passing
through a door –
to exchange
inner warmth for
outer cold,
the reassurance
of the old, for
the uncertainties
of the new;
the light, for
the darkness
of unknowing.

Do not resist
opening your door to
the unexpected caller;
desist from closing it
merely because you
fail to recognize
the stranger
waiting there.

This little piece was set to music in 2001 as
"Could but my Heart Respond"

Depression

The sun shines so
brightly. Could but my heart
respond! – but, within it, there are
shadows that not even the sun
can reach: shadows cast, not by
the sun, but by a dark despond.

Dies Horribilis

I woke in darkness –
darkness which couldn't
be relieved by switching on
a light, hunger, too, which
I couldn't satisfy
with food, pain
for which there was
no antidote, cold,
but no heat with which
to overcome it, my nostrils
filled with the stench of
decomposing matter, but
no means to dispose of it;
above all, no way of
transporting my
tormented being from
what seemed close to
Hell itself.

No, not Hell:
just life as it
would be, if
all the services,
performed day in,
day out, on my behalf
so unobtrusively
by my fellow man,
were suddenly to
be withdrawn.

E Mail

How can I thank you
for your email, and the
xxxxx's that, in such
generous measure,
not only ended it,
but began it, too?

   And all this at a
   time in life when
   xxxxx's (yes - and
   hugs as well) are in
   such short supply –
   deemed (maybe) "surplus
   to requirements" in the
   very elderly.

Like a box of choice
chocolates then, I shall
stash them away in a
safe corner of my heart,
whence I can help myself
to one (or more) –
"as required", on a
rainy day.

   Surely this is
   the right thing
   to do with a
   sudden, and
   unexpected
   wealth of
   xxxxx's?

Fiction - and Fact

You see, I had this dream –
well, daydream, really –
about a car that had been
stowed in an empty
aircraft hangar, the doors
then locked and sealed.
And I watched –
endlessly it seemed –
no longer an occupant
of Einstein's fourth
dimension, but of a zone
where time stood still:
hours, days, weeks and –
who knows? – even months
went by; and all that time
I was impelled never to
take an eye off the sealed
locks of those hangar doors.

    I dreamed on –
    to a time when, at last,
    officials reappeared
    (looking more like beings
    from another world), and
    broke the seals, swung wide
    the doors, and out came –
    no! – not a car, but an
    aeroplane, that immediately
    took to the air. And the car?
    It wasn't any longer there!

Fanciful? Agreed!
Daydreaming? Indeed! – cars
don't turn into aeroplanes
behind closed doors
(and what headlines,
if they did!).

    Yet caterpillars turn into
    butterflies, and we
    don't even turn
    a hair.

Flight of Fancy

It could be argued that we'd
met halfway, somewhere over
the Indian Ocean – or, maybe,
off the east coast of Africa? –
the very nature of our meeting
precluding the use of any
navigational system, from
humble sextant, to the
pin-point accuracy of GPS.

   What matter? We were well met! –
   albeit in the middle of nowhere –
   lost to the world, it might be said,
   as we exchanged news and views,
   and did our best to put the Universe
   to rights – the passage of time
   without meaning or
   measure.

That is, until I heard the clock in
his living room begin to chime the
hour, declaring that, for him, it
was eleven pm, for me mere
four o'clock. He bade me, then,
'Good Afternoon', and I bade *him*
'Goodnight', and, with the phone
back on its rest, I settled down –
alone – to an afternoon
cup of tea.

   And he? To an Australian
   nightcap, I suppose (whatever
   that might be).

Heavenly(?) Call Centre

'If you are calling about
a bereavement,
please press One.
If you are calling about
a row with your wife,
please press Two,
if you are calling about
an unanswered prayer,
please press Three,
if you are contemplating
suicide, please hold –
one of our angels
will be with you
as soon as possible.'
But following some
solemn music,
'We are sorry – all our angels
are busy at the moment.
You are in a queue.
Your call *is* important to us.
Please continue holding.'
More solemn music,
then, finally, 'We are sorry –
all our angels are busy still.
Please call back later.'

Horizons

My day has just begun
(or so I say), but –
what presumption!
Does *anyone* own *any* day,
save God? So, let's begin again,
with the day that God's just
given me, yet whose beginning,
I suspect, might be judged
anything but God-given
(the weathermen called it
'dull', and 'grey'; but –
one saving grace –
'the visibility good').

So, as I sit here quietly,
in contemplative mood,
gazing through my window,
the horizon, atop the line
of distant hills, is to be seen
"sharp as a razor's edge" –
above it the sky,
below it, the fields.
And beyond it?
Ah – to me (and fancifully,
in present mood), it hides
not space, but time:
not land, and yet more land ,
then sea, and land again, till,
circling the Earth, we arrive back
where we started, but the rest of
what I arrogantly called *my* day,
together with those yet to come,
be they few, or many, with
Eternity stretching
endlessly out of
sight – and
human
ken.

In The Park

Giants – their lives rooted in
a bygone age of crinolines
and sedan chairs, their heights,
and even girths measured in
tens of feet – standing, unmoved,
in the stiff breeze, as their candle
blossoms shed their fragile petals,
like so many snow flakes, to cloak
the green grass white:
giants, yes, but gentle –
their message a reminder
that, though winter be
scarce gone, yet is
Spring upon us now.

Lament

Dawn was waiting to greet us
as we wakened, twenty miles apart,
to meet later, when the sun,
sporting his brightest palette,
had finished his morning's work,
and overlaid the drab grey virgin
canvas of the first-light day with
tentative streaks of pearl pink;
and then, emboldened, flaunting
emerald green, with rich red —
shepherd's warning.

But, no shepherd he,
with whom I was to meet:
he sang his greeting to the
new-born day all too ignorant
of the warning — and the
appointment we were to keep.

(**F**or a bird killed in the early morning, whilst driving a car.)

Less Time – or Time-less?

"No time to stand and stare,"
no time to sit and be aware
that there's more to life than a
healthy heart, a
full stomach, and
money in the bank.

We jog enthusiastically,
and thereby (so we're told)
add to our lives merely
the time spent jogging.
('So you'd better enjoy it!'
a wag has said.) But –
spend that time simply
sitting, steeped in the
stillness of the Spirit,
and we could find we
had added Eternity
to our finitude
of days.

Monday Morning Blues

'Another day,
another week', but
'How time flies!' too trite
to add.

   Yet, it does more,
   much more than that:
   it *evaporates* as into
   thin air – or so it
   often seems,
   to me.

And I ask (as of water into steam)
'What is there left to show for it:
that last hour, last day, last week,
month, year; and – looming fast
for me – whole lifetime?'

   Indeed, time flies – and, yes,
   not worth the breath to say so;
   but, by that self-same token,
   is it not true that, soon, will
   Tuesday come?
                And –
   with it – a whole new
   ball game.

Mosquito

Mosquito,
need I have killed you? –
so wonderfully made,
with wings outstripping
the cunningest conception
of the aerodynamicist,
vibrating,
incredibly powered
by reflexes of nerve and muscle
concealed within the tiny nacelle
of your body;
buzzing,
propagating through the warm air
the fatal sound
that brought you to your end.

Those eyes, too,
multiple-facetted –
possessed,
not of the static, sterile beauty
of mere diamonds,
but purposeful –
monitoring the air about you
for likely enemies.

Yet did they fail to save you
from my low, lethal cunning: wings
divinely planned and fashioned,
nerve-muscle complexes,
multi-faceted
eyes, reduced –
all – to a mere
bloody smear
of biological matter,
on news-sheet
already besmirched
with overmuch indication of
Man's lack of understanding
of God's world.

Mosquito –
so fearfully, so wonderfully
made – need I have
killed you?

Mother and Child

Leg-weary,
lack-lustre, as she
pushed the pram, was it
homeward, to seek solace
in a long-awaited
cup of tea? – or was she
outward-bound, for the
Supermarket, and the
daily need to balance
the price tags against
a whole family
to feed?

    Work-weary,
    she made the pram
    (the baby, too) look like
    an encumbrance she could
    well have done without –
    the transition from
    live baby to dead weight
    insidious; the joy,
    the miracle of giving birth,
    for time being, quite forgot.

World-weary,
I watched with pristine
vision late acquired from
new things becoming old,
and old things
new:

    the baby seen as though
    first-born of all – first *ever*
    to grace this Earth of ours;
    a myriad of lifeless
    protons, neutrons, electrons
    (and all the rest), beloved
    of the physicist for
    their obedience to
    formulated rules, but –
    in a mother's womb –
    preposterously
    given life. Yes, *life!* –
    to become the child
    of which, rightly,
    she would be
    so proud;

    insidious, indeed,
    the transition from
    miracle, to mere
    mundane
    mood.

Murder in a Country Garden

It was as if an angry wasp
had been trapped inside
the microphone of a
public address system –
assaulting the ears with
its savage announcement,
and swamping the mind with
atavistic fears, gene-inscribed,
to muster the self-preserving
instinct against God knows
what invader of the
early morning air.

    Whence was it? And why
    the riveting demand
    to trace it to its source?
    What was it that
    had stopped me
    dead in my tracks,
    with urgent pause –
    insisting on an answer
    to incipient dread?

Fearfully,
I opened the door, and –
cautiously peering out –
saw two men, hell-bent on
murdering a friend of
many years: my neighbour's
walnut tree.

Newsnight

We played at soldiers – and
they paid us handsomely
for doing so. Not only that:
they had made a trestle
table-top, of simply *vast*
proportions, to serve as
an arena where we could
fight a simulated war.
What's more, they'd made
whole mountain ranges, seas,
and deserts (towns and
cities, too). And, as if that
weren't enough, there were
the most delightful model
tanks and aeroplanes –
with helicopter gun-ships, and
several battle cruisers, too!

We played,
and played, and
played – till we found it
hard to stop. And millions
watched, as we worked it out
(as best we could) how many
would be killed: a mere
ten thousand, were the
action simple, short,
and sharp? But, if the
factor of surprise (and not
a pleasant one, at that)
were lost, it might be
three times ten
to the fourth – or
was it fifth?
Never mind! –
what's in a factor of
ten, when it comes to
the casualties of war?

After all –
if they used gas, a hundred
thousand estimated dead
could be, indeed, conservative.
And, should biological warfare
ever become the name of
the game, or we went nuclear,
we couldn't rule out the
sixth, or even seventh
power of ten.

Actually –
sad to say –
for certain of the weapons
there just weren't enough
hard data on the "yield" (that's
numbers killed, of course):
you see, they haven't been
properly *tested* "in the field".
BUT – guess what! – by
tomorrow night (we think)
war might actually have
broken out, and we can
discuss the real thing:

"game on" in earnest, then!

(Written during the run-up
to the First Gulf War – 1990)

NOT in the January Sales...

A special offer, so special
that it's free; what's offered
special, too – and said to be
"beyond all understanding"...
So – to put it vulgarly –
what could be in it
for you and me?

   You'd never guess – not in
   a thousand years:
   it's *peace!*

But – I hear you say, 'What's hard
about *that* to understand?
Any numbskull – however dull –
could tell you what *peace* is:
no screaming kids around, nothing
boiling over on the stove, and
nobody knocking on the door
just when the baby needs
a nappy change. What could be
easier to understand
than *that?'*

   Ah – yes – but, just what did
   he mean to say? – I mean, the one
   who made the offer. Was it not
   of a new *kind* of peace? –
   peace that stays with you
   even when the saucepan
   has boiled dry, the baby's
   continuing, inconsolably, to
   cry – and you've just found out
   from "Google" exactly what
   that anxiously-awaited
   diagnosis might
   imply.

Now – and Then

It was hot –
not a time for seeking
new experiences –
and I lay on my back
in the garden, relaxing,
my mood vacant, though
far from pensive, as
eyes stared upward –
nothing in view, save
the infinite void
of a cloudless,
deep-blue sky.

   Suddenly, then,
   as from over my head,
   there came a seagull –
   gliding, wings
   rigid and motionless –
   so high that it seemed
   in another world from mine.

And, in that moment, as I
watched the sole occupant
of that timeless space,
it was as though I had
never seen a bird before –
its effortless, and seemingly
perpetual motion
sheer miracle
to ponder.

   So, too, must it have been,
   these long years since, as –
   supine in my pram –
   I saw, for first time ever,
   a bird gliding,
   high in the sky
   above me.

Alas, that I
should have had
to wait this long,
to see, again,
what I saw – and
as I saw it –
then.

Numbers Count More

Yes, it certainly hit
the headlines – and no,
it wasn't the first player
to win ten tennis Grand
Slams in a row, nor was it
the batsman who first reached
a thousand runs this year;
nor even the millionth
customer to darken
Ikea's doors whilst the
summer sales were on.

It's true that – whatever
the event – it had, of
necessity, to satisfy
an insatiable appetite
for multiples of ten.
So, indeed, it was the
hundredth that had focussed
the attention – "a milestone",
they were calling it, though
"*tomb*stone" might have been a
more appropriate word.

Again, it's true, they did
mention the ninety-ninth –
the ninety-eighth as well –
it could hardly have been
otherwise, since all three
had died in each other's
company – but it was
the *hundredth* one whose
death had made it headline
news: yes – the hundredth
to die in Afghanistan,
at the hands of the
Taliban. And – in truth –
there was a *fourth:* the one
who blew himself up to
kill the other three:
three for the price of
one, in the market-place
of death.

So – what *was* it about the
hundredth? Was *his* death
in some way extra-*special?*
And did the parents of
the ninety-ninth suffer
that much less because
their son – as he fell –
fell *one short* of
the hundredth?

Ask them.

One Day, the Same as Any Other?

Yet another day, its bare bones
no different from any other –
and the same old clouds hiding a
would-be sun.

For sure, others won't have noticed
the difference: it's June, and the
seventh day of the month, which,
as it happens, is a Thursday –
you can't get more mundane than that.
Yet (did you guess then?), yes, it's my
birthday: one more milestone in my
life – and a massive one at that –
the end of another year of
my allotted span; and, at the
age of ninety three, there can but
be mere handful more
to come.

But, to the man who's just gone by,
walking his dog, it's still just a
Thursday in early June, in the
year Two Thousand and Seven
(and a very dull one,
at that).

------------ **Plain Ordinary?** ------------
(A Thought Experiment)

Should you,
perchance,
be one of those
who think this life of ours
is unremarkable, then you
need to think again.

Still sitting in your chair,
imagine your living room
no longer there, and then
the rest of your cosy little
house; as well, the road
in which it stands, the
town, for which the road
serves as an artery
(or, maybe, mere vein);
the country, too, which
claims you as a citizen,
and even planet Earth,
of which your homeland
is just a small hunk of
its creaking crust –
imagine *all that*
removed:

no sitting room,
(that warm, snug womb),
no street – every inch of it
so comfortingly familiar;
no town from which
you can drive away in your
four by four, knowing that,
in due course, you'll arrive at
some other place, where
kith and kin will greet you
with a friendly face; and –
beyond – no more
the welcoming
sound of sea's
slow slop on a
some familiar
shore.

With none of these
any longer
disposed,
reassuringly,
between you
and the infinitudes
of Space (whose
very existence
their interposition
has, hitherto,
enabled you
for the most part
to ignore):

with *none* of them
any longer there,
imagine just *you* –
stripped of all
those comforting
accoutrements of
life right down to
the bare bones,
so to say:
just *you*,
afloat
in your armchair,
in Space so immense
that even the existence
of countless galaxies
of unnumbered –
and, indeed,
innumerable –
stars, leaves it looking
largely empty,
still –

aware thus,
at long last,
that you were born,
not merely into a
modest house in a
humble street of an
insignificant town in a
pint-sized country on this
little old planet Earth,
but into the infinitudes
of a Universe of which
we may yet turn out to be
the sole inhabitants –

could life ever again
seem "plain ordinary"
to you?

Platform Parting

The train slows to a standstill –
and hedgerows, trees, and
green fields give way to
station notices, and hoardings
advertising beer, toothpaste, and
the latest in breakfast cereals;
a sea of waiting faces
appear against a backdrop
of Cafeteria, "Left Luggage",
porters, and the rest.

  The diesel hums, impatient
  of leave-takings spun out
  on the platform; and thin blue
  wisps of fuel smoke
  provoke the nostrils,
  educing uneasy
  memories of
  more momentous
  partings, now
  long past.

Just then,
two pairs of eyes
met, two pairs of hands
clasped, two pairs of lips
touched – and Cafeteria,
"Left Luggage",
porters, and
the rest of the
mundane motley
peopling the platform, fell
out of Time, and –
briefly – into
Eternity.

  (mid-1950s)

Poisoned Chalice

She was a bright young thing,
and no doubt meant well, too,
as she stooped, buckling
her knees to level with a
beggar squatting, cross-legged,
on the pavement, in that
cold, damp place.

   I envied her ability to bend her
   knees so readily, and, more so,
   her desire to greet that blotchy,
   bleary, grime-stained beggar,
   face to face.

She fumbled in her handbag,
whilst he looked on, expectantly –
I pondering, meantime, what value
coin could match such fellow-feeling.

   At last she found what she had
   fumbled for, and gently
   proffered it, not to hands,
   but lips – a
   cigarette:

   her good deed
   for the day...

Poles Apart

The view from my window,
though unpretentious, is yet
engaging, its line of low hills
inviting speculation as to
what lies beyond the skyline,
hanging from which a veritable
patchwork of fields, sewn together
by hedgerows – for all the world
like the knitted green and yellow
squares of a bedspread, hung out
to dry in the sunshine that
followed the morning showers.

  Be that as it may, yet am I
  well aware of what has been there
  since the day my eyes first lighted
  on the scene – just yards from my
  window, that inescapable
  telephone pole: a black stripe – a
  vicious swipe – from top to bottom of
  the view, severing the skyline,
  ripping through the patchwork of
  corn-yellow and cattle-grazing green,
  and bulldozing its way down through
  the valley that lies between.

But then, I look again, and
see what I have also seen
numberless times before: the
graceful catenary of wire
draped between the top of
that brutally obtrusive,
all-pervasive, creosoted
wooden pole and the corner
of my house – the vital first link
in a chain of electronic
wizardry (including a
satellite parked miles up in the
sky) that enables me to talk
to my friend nine thousand miles,
and more, beyond that horizon-
cum-clothesline that stands
'twixt him and me.

  Obtrusive? – yes –
  but an outsize
  in magic wands.

Privilege - at a Price

It hasn't even "sentimental" value,
nor could it ever be regarded as
an heirloom, to feature in my will –
less still, come under the hammer
of the auctioneer. In truth,
it doesn't even *belong* to me –
I just make quarterly payments
for the privilege of having it
to wear.

  It's not really a necklace –
  a pendant, I suppose –
  pricey, but by no means
  priceless; but, to me,
  precious indeed, and I
  would not, could not,
  willingly, be parted from it.
  You see – should I but
  feel the slightest twinge,
  or fall, and fail to find my
  feet again, then, one push on
  my pendant (it sports a
  little button), and whatever
  aid I need will come, and
  that in mere matter of
  minutes.

Yet, truth is that for
the price of such a
privilege a Third World
family could, each and
every quarter, be
provided with –
yes, wait for it –
two goats.

  And, the tally
  to date? – a herd of
  more than eighty. And
  I haven't even pressed
  that button
  once...

Reduced to a Pulp

Had I but known
I could have intervened –
and saved at least a few
(among several hundreds)
from a violent end.

None of them a stranger
to my deepest thoughts – all
privy to my greatest sorrows,
each, a witness to my direst
pain – they were almost
part of me; to renew
the acquaintance of
but one of them a source
of strength, should courage
wane.

Those who bear the burden
of their untimely end –
though, supposedly,
custodians, were yet
prepared to sacrifice
their protégés for a
trivial monetary gain –
wholly disregardful
of the investment
I had made in them:
not of money, but of
my very self.

Hard indeed, it is, to
believe that the hundreds of
copies remaining, of a book
in which I had bared my soul –
shared the worst and best
moments of my life – had,
with not a word of warning,
been summarily *pulped*:

I, too, with them –
or so it seemed.

(In 1994 my book "Your Sort of Courage", was published. I had written it as a tribute to Mary, my wife, who died in 1988, after 20 years of serious disability, so courageously borne. In 2005, when submitting an order for further copies of the book, I discovered that, without consulting me, the publishers had pulped a remainder of several hundred.)

Riches

They were walking
hand in hand, and
though it would seem
it was only a hand
they had in hand,
it was more than all
the world's wealth
put together –
did they but know.

But, perhaps they did...

S. A. D.

Icy-cold, day broke,
the sky afire, glorious
in its yellow-gold – my
spirit victorious over its
S.A.D.-based blues.

  But now,
  just one hour on, it rains
  outside my window, and
  inside my heart.

Yet, still does
my dampened spirit
bask in the afterglow
of a sky that was so
briefly brave, bold,
yellow-gold, in the
icy-cold –

just before
it rained.

Second Sight

I looked, with eyes
unseeing, on a
winter scene, the trees
stripped bare, their branches
black against a threatening sky.
Yet was I oblivious
of the pattern they
traced – outstripping
the beauty even of
their pristine, springtime
foliage to come.

   It was December,
   my spirit at its lowest
   ebb, with eyes for nought
   save that which would confirm
   my morbid mood.

But then,
I looked again,
and this time saw
a magnolia tree
in bud.

Seeing Things

It appeared, as if from nowhere –
one moment not, the next moment
there – waving briskly, through my
kitchen window, desperate, it seemed, for
my attention: thin and supple,
a spindly branch, wrested by the wind
from the heart of a neighbour's tree,
bent – quite literally – on a game of
"Peek-a-boo";

  but – not for long: the wind, changing,
  bent it lower still, and, moments later
  it was swaying from side to side,
  for all the world like a metal detector,
  gently scanning the lawn for
  buried treasure.

Wind veering then, and metal detector
had turned policeman, waving down
an errant motorist; sudden gusts, and
the policeman vanished as quickly as
he had come – and in his place
a conductor, flamboyantly
directing an orchestra in
a movement marked
"Allegro agitato".

  But, as suddenly, the wind was gone,
  and I was left, alone, with the
  hand of a beggar – outstretched
  in silent plea.

Seeking and Finding

To find,
it is better
to be already
seeking: to find,
without seeking,
is to risk
stumbling over
what you find –
and even
getting hurt.

Shopping for the Future?

I sat, awaiting my turn
at the Surgery. as she
walked in briskly, and
straight up to Reception.
And, so it seemed, she'd
brought her shopping
with her – the basket
shaped like a miniature
coracle, its handle so
long that had the floor been
water it would almost
have been afloat:

    in fact, so near the floor
    that she hardly seemed aware
    of it – less still its contents –
    in her eagerness to confirm
    the appointment with her doctor.
    'A cabbage and some potatoes,'
    I pondered, idly, 'and, maybe,
    a head of celery, too?'

In truth, there *was* no shopping;
no coracle either, but a *cradle* –
and in it the newest of
new-born babies.

    Times are, when we feel
    the weight of the world
    on our shoulders – but
    what if we have the
    whole of the future
    dangling from one arm?

Sixty-four Thousand Dollar Question

Shapeless
(it could be deemed),
and angular
in the extreme –
no symmetry,
and colour mostly
a drab grey.
Big – yes: *that*
would be the
understatement
of the year –
but it's *small* that's
beautiful (or so
they say).

How come, then,
mountains take my
breath away?

Talk ad Infinitum

It costs just threepence an hour –
a twentieth of a penny for
each minute of my life.

    Can you see that penny,
    and the tiny pile of filings
    shaved off to make a
    twentieth of the whole –
    each minute that I live?

Well – believe it as you will
(or not!) – it's all that I pay
for the opportunity to
speak to whomsoever I
choose, at any time, and in
any one of a myriad of
places, spread out across
the globe.

    The scientist – perpetrator
    of many a mixed blessing, and,
    occasionally, unmitigated
    curse – need feel of this
    but swelling pride; as well,
    the warmth of gratitude of
    this erstwhile solitary soul,
    miraculously enabled, now,
    to give voice, round
    the world.

The format of this handful of deceptively simple little verses was originally employed in a poem called "Operations Research", the name given in the Second World War to a new branch of mathematics specifically concerned with making the pursuit of war more "efficient". A paper employing these methods was published in which the letter "y" was actually used for "yield" – " to stand for men in battle killed", as my poem had it. The original poem was lost, but this poem, along the same lines, was written in the 1980s, on hearing the then Chancellor of the Exchequer counter the bankruptcy statistics merely by setting them against the statistics of new businesses being created.

The Advantage of Abstraction

'In algebra', the teacher said,
'we deal with things much better,
by simply placing in their stead
an algebraic letter.

'By this device, with power imbued,
we are in fact enabled
to calculate the magnitude
of quantities so labelled.

'For businesses new-formed, an "n",
for bankruptcies, a "b";
should "n" but "b" exceed - why, then! -
forget the misery!

'The beauty of the method's plain,
for when with symbols dealing,
a "b" 's a "*b*", and it is vain
to think that it has feeling.'

The Butterfly

It looked as fragile as
a wisp of smoke, as
it first flew into view –
kept airborne by those
frail and gently flapping
wings. Yet did its very
fragility seem a
befitting – even
inevitable – feature
of its unsurpassable
beauty, which, just then,
it was sharing with me,
and with God,
alone.

How come
I was so privileged?

The Christmas Tree

Throughout
the festival,
it had stood
in the window
in all its finery,
its crowning glory
a silver star, whence
a string of fairy lights
had spiralled downwards
in ever-widening circles,
for all the world like
the hoops of a crinoline;
bright baubles at the end of
every branch serving as
giant sequins, to enhance
the impression of a lady
decked out in her
festive best.

We worked
slowly, reluctantly,
taking our time:
first the star –
disentangling
its hidden stalk, and
committing it to the
waste paper basket
(did ever a star suffer
such a humiliating end?).

And then the baubles,
their fate less ignominious:
blown glass and silvered,
they found themselves nesting –
like a clutch of eggs – back in
their box, for another
Christmastide.

And – finally – the fairy lights,
their shape-defining circles
unravelled from the tree,
to be – like the baubles –
stowed away, for another
(Christmas) day.

There remained the tree –
rootless, stripped bare,
and thankfully unaware
of its fate: to be
propped up against
the dustbin, till the next
refuse collection day.

The Economics of Giving

'Give more
on Mother's Day,'
the Advert said –
but omitted to state
the reason why
it was offering
the advice.

Which was?
But of *course!* –
it takes the expertise
of an advertising agent
to turn gift into
a profit

The Flowers that Don't Bloom
In the Spring

The daffodils, breaking cover,
have headed heavenward,
towards their DNA-determined
destination, there to burst bud,
and trumpet in bright yellow tones
the triumph of Spring's resurrection
over Winter's death.

Were that
yet so:

no host can I boast
in my humble plot,
nor can my heart
with pleasure fill –
less still dance
with the daffodils,
as did the heart of
Grasmere's bard.

True – for *him*
they were the ever-faithful
harbingers of Spring, but,
for *us,* who knows, of what? –
when we have yet
to see the end of
January, and daffodils,
blossoming presently,
can but be
bad news.

The Flowers

Bright red and
deep crimson, frilly-skirted,
they looked for all the world like
ballerinas arrayed in
tutus, poised and ready
for the dance.

And so they stayed, as I
tended them day by day,
until, one morning,
I found them – stems
arched over – bowing
deep to an unseen
audience, their
performance
at an end.

The Man Next-Door

I know,
for a fact,
that, surreptitiously,
he keeps close watch
on my windows, and deduces
what my every movement is,
from which light is on,
and which one off,
which curtain drawn,
and which one not:
indeed, he must
know just when I
get up, *and* when I
go to bed...

    Conscious, too, am I, of the
    fact that – as cat watches
    mouse – he makes due note of
    when I leave the house, and
    when, precisely,
    I return.

Came the day, then,
when a taxi arrived,
and went again
without me; and,
ten minutes later,
he was knocking
on my door.
'That taxi I saw –
it came and went
without you,' he said,
adding, anxiously –
in his rich West Country
accent – 'Are you *alright?'*

(How reassuring! –
to know that I am watched
so unobtrusively, and
with such neighbourly
concern.)

The Virtues of Necessity

I was like the
owner of a boat
who – taking one look
at the inclement weather –
had decided it was not
the morning to put to sea.

Eventually, though,
for better or for worse –
and summoning
such determination
as I could muster –
I clambered out of bed
and drew back the curtains
on the day that, willy-nilly,
awaited me, to find a
man, *his* day well on,
laboriously picking up
the rubbish, bit by each
single bit, from the
pavement outside
my house.

And I fell to envying
the sheer necessity that
had given him no option
but to get up, and get on
with his day – bring
what it may.

Too Much for Granted

It all began
with the baby
in a pram, seen as if
first ever from a
mother's womb. And then
the seagull, gliding into view,
the two of us, as it were,
sole occupants of a
private world; the butterfly
as well – just God and I, sharing
its inimitable beauty:
baby, seagull, and butterfly –
each, in its own way
witness to the truth that life
can, and should, be lived
"new every day".

Yet, living it round the clock,
day in, day out, we take
too much for granted – from
the merest mite in a
bag of flour, to an elephant
in Africa; from sub-atomic
particles, to the myriads of
stars and galaxies, and the
infinitudes of space;
we give more thought to
tomorrow's shopping list
than to the wonders of
the Universe – backdrop
to this life of ours,
the greatest wonder
of them all.

Would that we
could live each day
as if newborn! – to see
our lives, at each and every
waking dawn, as if with
first-time-open
eyes.

Two Women

They sat, still as
the two figures of
a statue, and —
in a public place —
as much on view;
the older,
(I was sure)
the mother of
the younger, who,
leaning forward, was
holding her head
low, and motionless,
between her hands.

I watched,
discreetly,
from a distance,
drawn — and held —
by the expression
on the older woman's
face: the quintessence of
a mother's compassion
for her child; her vigil
the more harrowing
for the silence she
deemed it necessary
to keep.

And,
as I watched,
it seemed that,
suddenly, a
very public place
had become, instead,
a very private one.

And I left,
as it were on
tip-toe.

Village By The Sea

The steep cliff, presiding
over pebbled beach,
falls gently, inland,
where wooded lee
borders the tumbling
stream, eager to
lose itself in the
open bosom of
the grey-green sea.
The pebbles, under
the relentless urge
of rolling, white-capped
breakers, ebb and flow
with endless murmur
in the sea's slow surge –
mesmeric music of the
undertow, casting its spell,
far from the rain-swept face
of craggy cliffs, on
winding village roads:
the measured beat of
life lived at gentler pace
among the chalky combes,
and thatched abodes.
On these –
fluorescent green –
the lichen grows,
contrasting starkly
with the staring white
of new-built homes –
their rectilinear rows
refusing to be lost
to sight.
Beside the stream
the willows sway,
leaf-bare, yet adding
welcome colour splash
to drab grey palette
of a misty day; but
rivalled, even so, by
finch's brilliant flash,
who, with the coal tit
and the jenny wren,
is busy in the hedgerow
by the inn.

Inside,
a plenitude
of goodly smells
pervades the air –
holds captive
motley crowd of
humankind, as each,
to neighbour, tells his
cautionary tale,
both long and loud, and
sips his consolation
from a glass;
a refugee from time
and outside state,
he lets the world and
all its problems pass.
I order modest
ploughman's lunch,
and wait.

Outside,
the road rolls gently past,
to climb towards the church;
and in its leisured course runs
by the forge to sound of
anvil's chime – like clank of
ghostly chains, from time when
clop of horse and crunch of
wooden wheels were sole
disturbers of the peace,
as men laboured, and their
business plied: no ghost
the flame's gleam, as the
hammer pounds the iron, and
the bright sparks fly!

And,
above it all,
the ancient church, foursquare,
stands sentinel – with graves
that quietly tell of those who,
these long centuries since,
did bear their brutish day,
yet living, dying well:
those who, unknown, unsung,
yet left their imprint here –
where we, like them, can
dream our dreams, and
share their immortality.

What If...?

When I was young,
my elders used to say,
'Now leave it
as you found it' –
where "it" was a box
of my favourite toys,
a pile of neat-stacked
story books, or a drawer,
full of clothes, destined
to serve as props, in a
game of "make-believe".

But, what if "it"
is a whole planet:
of grassy meadows
and tumbling streams,
of towering mountains
and rolling seas,
of leafy hedgerows
and blossoming trees;
of children who think it
will all stay the same
for them –

but it won't?

What, On Earth, Are We Doing?

Homes don't just
happen: long before
they are bricks and
mortar (or even
just mud and straw)
they are somebody's
dream – their castle
in the air.

　But the castle
　an Englishman deems
　his home to be – far from
　airborne – is rooted and
　grounded on Planet Earth
　(fit and able to support,
　not only its foundations,
　but his wife and
　children, too).

And – let's face it –
though neglect might
ruin the ramparts,
or even topple the tower,
there would seem to be
nothing an Englishman
(or anyone else) could do
that would threaten its
billions-of-years-old
foundations.

　Believe it or not
　(and you'd better) –
　it's not the castle, *or*
　the way it was built that
　threatens the foundations, it's
　the way he *inhabits* it now:
　the way he comes and goes
　about his work and play,
　endlessly, to and fro,
　frittering away the
　energy stored deep in
　Mother Earth, and
　poisoning the planet
　even as he does so;
　till time may come
　(and the clock ticks
　louder by the day)
　when there is no longer
　anywhere to go –
　to *or* fro –

or anyone
to do so.

When Imitation Doesn't Flatter

Theirs is a beauty
all but outstripping
that which they strive
to emulate, and long
outlasts it: a beauty
that needs no sustenance
to maintain its eye-catching,
spell-binding, blemish-free
appearance – untouched by
the likes of stretch marks,
and exempt from any need
of soothing, moisturizing, or
restorative creams.

   Production-engineered, and
   mass-produced, they flaunt
   themselves on markets' shelves.
   Go on! Splash out! – and
   buy yourself a bunch
   of blush-red roses,
   cloth-petalled, and
   plastic-leaved.

And take them home and
prop them up in a vase:
no need of water, or
any other form of TLC –
except, maybe, an
occasional going-over
with the business end
of a vacuum cleaner,
as the dust gathers
over the weeks, months,
and – who knows? –
even years. What's that?
You don't like hoovering
a bunch of flowers?
Not to worry! – they
wouldn't quail – even
in a force-nine gale.

              *   *   *

There was a moment when,
of a sudden, I came upon –
no – *not* a host of
golden daffodils, but a
bunch of somesuch pretend-
flowers, attempting to
brighten the cloddy earth
of a fresh-dug grave;

but their brash attempt
at artificial immortality
seemed strangely
out of place.

Wind from Russia

I wandered, lonely, in a
crowd, my body close to
home, my spirit far away,
tossed, hither and thither,
on a sea of restless thoughts
whipped up by the winds of
change – threatening to
cast me, high and dry, on
a far-off, unfamiliar
shore.

   Suddenly, then,
   there came the sound of
   distant music, wafted on the
   morning breeze, bright, bold, and –
   yes! – *brazen.* (It was played by
   a brass ensemble!)

Jostled by the crowd,
I traced it to its source –
five men – *their* bodies also
far from home, but their
spirits (unlike mine, just then)
having both local habitations
and a name:
two trumpets,
a horn,
a trombone
and a tuba.
What joy sprang
from the mere sight
of their gleaming
bells and valves, and
convoluted tubing!

   Their repertoire ranged
   far and wide. What matter
   that it was familiar, and
   sometimes near to trite?
   The Wind from Russia had
   out-blown the winds of change,
   and my spirit – no longer
   storm-tossed and adrift –
   came home again, to music
   heard for what it was: voices,
   not just from Russia,
   but from Heaven
   itself.

THE SPIRIT

CONTENTS

A Matter of Hardware and Software

Puny, and
preposterously
vulnerable: so much
software among the gigantic
hunks of hardware out there,
in the Universe, we humans
seem about as significant
as a subatomic particle
in a grain of mustard seed.

So, what of it –
all that hardware?
To be sure, it doesn't
come cheap. And why
so much? – an *infinite*
amount, in an *infinitude*
of space – yet (it would seem)
contributing little or nothing
towards Life elsewhere,
or here, on planet Earth.

The amounts of Einstein's
Energy and Time beyond
imagining, there lies
buried within creation
on such scale deep
rhyme, and even deeper
reason, that needs
be pondered well:
was that much creation
what it took, to enable
this grain of Life?

A Visitor to Breakfast

It had a head, a trunk, and a metasoma,
and, like others of its kind, an "exoskeleton"
assembled on the outside, with no covering
of skin, muscles, or body tissues;

its head wondrously equipped, with
multiple eyes and (so-called) "feelers" –
actually organs of smell – the bodies
of it and its fellows emitting "pheromones",
smelling variously, and, by means of which
it had communicated complex information
to its companions; a pair of pincers, too,
I almost said *adorned* the head, but,
no ornament these – employed to dig,
defend, and carry food many times its
body weight.   And, just inside its mouth
a pocket in which it had stored food, to
give to any of its companions,
found to be in need.

Its trunk had had all of six legs attached to it,
at the end of each a sharp claw, enabling it
to climb, and hang onto things; and the near-
miraculous coordination of all six legs,
working together, had enabled it to run
at the equivalent – for us humans – of
full sixty miles an hour.

More sinisterly, its metasoma had comprised
a poison sac, its stinger capable of inflicting
a very painful little wound even on us humans,
billions of times its size.

Minus lungs – it had breathed through
pores in its skin – no blood vessels either:
a tube-like heart conveying colourless blood,
literally, "from top to toe", and, like an interior
decorator, coating the whole of its inside
with the colourless stuff – retrieving it then,
and taking it back to the head again.
And, as for nerves, it had a kind of
spinal cord (minus the spine), with
branches to all its different body parts.

Yes! You're *right!* It was an *ant* – out for
the ant's equivalent of a morning jog across
my breakfast table, blissfully unaware that
it was trespassing – for which, according to
my book, the punishment was death by
summary justice, administered then and there,
by the ball of my thumb: a three-dimensional
manifestation of Life, in near-miraculous
miniature, reduced in the instant to a lifeless
two – what I had done, the biological equivalent
of taking a razor to a van Gogh canvas,
or dropping a bomb on the
Taj Mahal.

According to the Child

Said Christ, 'To enter the Kingdom,
hard, indeed, shall it be, except that
like a child you come, your spirit
innocent of pride, your heart of envy free.'

Poor in worldly goods are we – though,
unencumbered thus, we come, our
glory trailing – rich yet be, for life's
true wealth we know. Nor grudge we
bear, withhold nor love, from whomso
love does proffer.

But, hard the call: too simple, far,
our Gospel, for grown-up mind
make out its sense, so – sorrowing –
go they hence.

No magic wand is ours: such powers
we have do in our very weakness
lie – no threat, thus, can we be,
save to your unreadiness
to love.

Nor say the time not yet at hand
('We needs must weighty matters tend').
The time is ever ripe to love, and ever ripe
the time to mend. But, 'ware! Our very
weakness is the ground wherein, already,
are the seeds of suffering sown:
children of sorrow we, acquainted, too,
with grief. So, as you follow, tread with
care, for friends (yes, friends – not enemies)
will say that you are 'out your mind'.

Yet, banish fears! And dry your tears! –
for the sun in God's sky has risen high,
to show where the treasure is hid –
and found: deep buried in your heart
it lies, 'neath the weight of grown-up
fears – of lingering shadows from
the past, and future's sombre loom –
as the sense of doom, firstborn
of fear, destroys the Eternal Now,
where, to live, the Child alone
knows how.

Active Service

I wasn't conscripted,
I volunteered – by giving,
in friendship, all I had
to give; I didn't know
I'd need a bullet-proof vest.

One day, at close range,
my friend shot me
through the heart
of my deepest feelings;
the self that I was,
dying a lingering death,
and, finally, laid to rest.

A new, and fragile self
emerged – like a phoenix
from the ashes – to find
that, unwittingly, it was
in the front line of a battle,
ongoing since human life
began – its objective? –
to wring out of suffering
a meaning consistent
with the existence of the
rings of Saturn, and the
dimensions of the Milky Way.
It was a commission which,
more than willingly,
I would have relinquished –
simply to find myself
back in Blighty again.

Alas, all too soon,
I discovered that – within
the system of governance
that covered such bulky items
as Saturn and the Milky Way,
and, yes, suffering, too –
no arrangements had been made
for conscientious objectors,
less still, deserters. So,
like it or not, I was in it
"for the duration". Worse still,
there was no prospect of
going on leave: one was,
perforce, required to engage
in combat "round the clock";
no truce, either, on Sundays,
Bank Holidays, or the days
set aside to celebrate the
lives of saints – in fact,
"no respite" the
order of the day.

Soon, I was engulfed in the
isolation of the battlefield, as
I visualized the rest of the world
about its business as usual –
eating, drinking, and making merry –
blissfully unaware that tomorrow
they might be joining me.
I felt like a railway coach,
uncoupled from the train of Life
and shunted into a siding,
whilst the rest of the coaches
(it seemed to me) went
rolling on into the sunset –
and endless revelry.

Strange questions, then,
I found myself asking–
'Were *they* living life to the full,
or was I? Was life about
asking the big questions –
answers forthcoming, or not –
or merely enjoying the answers
to the trivial ones?'

At first, I would readily
have settled for the latter –
more than willing to leave to
others the answers to the
big ones – only to find that
I had no option: find the big
answers, or spiritually *wilt,*
and die.

'Why?' I asked,
'why was *I* embattled thus? –
committed to the task
of finding ultimate answers
to ultimate questions, whilst
others were reclining on
distant, sun-drenched beaches, or
idly lobbing pebbles into a pond?'
That was yet another question,
demanding yet another answer –
but I was near-spent.

Yet – the battle
well and truly joined –
I found still one more question
demanding my attention
(time-honoured, this one):
'Why, for goodness' sake (yes! –
indeed, for *goodness'* sake),
does God allow suffering
at all?'

It's the question that the
atheist can neatly sidestep,
leaving it fairly and squarely
on the believer's plate.
'Where *was* God,
and what was he *doing*,
when that suicide bomber
blew himself up, with
an unknown number
of others?

Was he *really* auditioning
a new angelic choir whilst
that child was being savagely
beaten and battered to death?
And – much nearer home –
did he have his back turned,
so that he merely *heard* that shot,
oblivious of its consequences,
for me?' The answers
needed to be good.

For many months
they were anything *but*:
'Suffering is the price
you have to pay to
wipe the slate clean of
past misdemeanours' –
or – 'It's simply a process
of toughening up, like work-
hardening a piece of steel';.
Or, again – 'Life is still
evolving – there is bound
to be suffering "on the way" '.
Whichever the case,
it amounted to a God
absent from his creation –
and, for that matter,
absent from me,
in my moment
of direst need.

Strangely, then,
at those very moments –
moments when, of a certainty,
it would seem I should have been
at my most desolate, my most
forsaken – I came to feel, indeed,
somehow to *know,* that I was not
alone: that I was *not* adrift on an
empty sea, but a crewman on a
boat called "Me", with
sure hands on
the tiller.

Trite?
Trivial?
Vintage Victorian
sentimentalism?
Then think again –
the implications providing
nothing less than the answer
to the question over-arching all:
'Where *was* God when the
suicide bomber blew himself up,
with who-knows-how-many others?'

So rooted and grounded
is each and every human life
in him, that, yes, he was
there – being blown up
with the rest.

And the baby?
He was there, too –
beaten, battered, and
crucified,
anew.

And that bullet
through my heart?
Yes – that's right –
it went through
his heart
too.

Alas: As Was – As Is

A hungry man could not
have seized more avidly on
long-awaited food than did
my mind upon the spoken word –
tossed toward me by a radio,
half-ignored, and only, thus,
half-heard. 'Actually,' the man had
said, 'I'm more optimistic now,
about Christmas'.

 Would that I had heard
 the context of this affirmation
 of faith revitalized, which had
 opened the sluice gates of my
 pent-up heart, releasing a flood
 of new hope – of a return to
 Christmas as it was
 meant to be.

But *hush!* The man himself
is spelling out his reasons now –
for hoping for better things:
for the new life that a
pre-Christmas run-away
spending spree would breathe
into a lacklustre
economy...

---------------- All at Sea ----------------
A Parable for the Twenty-first Century

It was only a small cloud –
near the horizon, too –
no bigger than a man's hand,
as they say, so,
why all the fuss?
They were cruising along
contentedly,
enjoying the sunshine,
and the salty spray –
you know the feeling:
sunset's an eternity away,
why plan the day?

No concerns, either,
about navigation:
with modern techniques
(they had been told)
their position known to
within a matter of yards;
nor were there any misgivings
as to how they should proceed
to their intended destination:
all was set fair –
or so it seemed.

Admittedly,
there were those
who expressed unease
about the cloud,
claiming that,
small though it was,
it was destined
to get much bigger,
presaging dire things –
sooner rather than later, too –
and their advice was to stop
distracting one another
with fun things
(like deck quoits,
and splashing around
in the swimming pool)
and to concentrate on
what was really urgent now:
an immediate change of
course. The consequences
of ignoring their advice,
they said, would be to
expose the ship to
unprecedented
conditions that it had
not been designed
to withstand, spelling
certain disaster, for
one and all.

But, sad to say,
among the passengers were
some who had a vested
interest in leaving things
as they were (business deals,
along the way) – no change of
course for them, they said.

So – they sailed on,
captain, crew, and passengers
somewhat reassured by the
thought that their first landfall
was, in fact, due, the very next day.
Even the scaremongers
(as they had quickly been dubbed)
rested more easily in their bunks
that night, in the knowledge
that at least there would be time
for further thought on how to
avert catastrophe.

Strangely, then, they all awoke –
quite suddenly – with a feeling of
having grossly overslept; of the
world being a different place from
the one they had fallen asleep in –
moreover, the change, they sensed,
had not been for the better.
And it was hotter –
much hotter.

With their binoculars, then,
they anxiously scanned the horizon
for first signs of what the brochures
had assured them would be
an idyllic island, where they could
while away yet more time.

But they looked in vain.

And – another thing –
there was no trace
of that patch of cloud.
Whatever it had portended must
(they said) already have taken place
whilst they had slept.
And why, they were asking,
was there no sign of the
island?

At first, there were snide remarks
about the flaunted accuracy
of the navigational system –
that is, until someone,
taking a second look, said
he could see the top of a tree
just above the surface of the
sea: there *must* have been a
Tsunami-style earthquake in the
night, he said.

It was a natural enough
conclusion, the alternative
unthinkable – that the island
had stayed where it was,
whilst the sea had risen up
and drowned it.
It was – for them –
the stuff of dreams;
or even nightmares.

(But that was only because
they had been asleep
so long.)

An Autumn Morning in 1970

She lay, a coat draped over her –
nearby, the dented bonnet of a car
which had ended her shopping
before it had begun.

   It was England –
   on a sunny autumn morning –
   and she had fallen like
   an autumn leaf:
   perhaps as dead.

And I thought of Vietnam,
half a world away, where
women (babies, too) could,
on the short, sharp burst of
a mortar bomb, litter the
stricken streets – not just
one, but a whole heap of
autumn leaves; and,
like them, to be
carted away
as so much litter –
waste products
of a war:

   at least, in England,
   someone cared enough
   to cover her with a coat.

------------- 'As It Were' - and As It Was ------------

So – you thought it was
'a figure of speech,'
justified, of course
(as you would say),
by the need to
emphasise that
events had taken
such a tragic turn.

I have to admit,
I thought so, too –
I mean, that it was
hyperbole – and
never *intended*
to be taken as
literal truth. That is,
until that moment
when I typed the words
into 'Google', to
find – amazingly –
that it was *true*:
you *could* sweat blood –
but the circumstances
so extreme that,
down the centuries,
the reported cases
had struggled to reach
double figures in the
Journals – medical or
otherwise: the Bible
the first, and the
first-ever case
on record that of
Christ.

And now it has a name,
inevitably concealing
the ultimate in suffering
that needs be plumbed,
to add one's very blood
to common sweat.

Haemathidrosis –
none less – the word
lacking in Luke's lexicon,
the condition beyond
his ken: physician
though he was,
he simply said,
'his sweat was
"as it were"
great drops of
blood, falling
to the ground'.
But what if
he had known
that "as it were"
was as it was? –
what then?

And, what *now*,
of you and me? – you,
who thought it
simply a well-chosen
figure of speech, and I,
who deemed it
justifiable hyperbole.
What do we do
with the truth that
bloody sweat reveals –
that God, in Christ,
chose to suffer,
to its very limit,
what it means
to be a man?
I mean, we can't
just ignore it, can we?

Or *can* we?

At the End of My Tether?

Of a sudden – and
as in a nightmare –
I saw my concern
for countless numbers
of my fellow humans
as a single – and
woefully weak – thread,
from which dangled,
precariously,
the whole gamut
of Mankind's troubles;
a thread unequal to the
burden, and strained
to breaking point.

But then, the burgeoning
nightmare turned into
a dream-by-day, in which
the thin threads of concern –
each for another –
of many millions,
formed themselves
into a plaited rope,
whose strength –
far exceeding
the sum total of
its solitary strands –
was match for
any moment,
even of Man's
direst hour.

But, as dream became
a casualty of day's
cold light, the question
inevitably raised
its ugly head: were there
enough left, of those
who could, and would
be prepared to
plait?

Before Her Time?

Resting in her palm,
a pebble, the size of
a hazelnut – and, no, it
wasn't just the other day
on Brighton beach: it was
in Norwich, seven centuries
since. And her name? –
it was Julian.

Unusual, you think? –
I mean – that a mere pebble
in a woman's hand should
find a place in history.
But, you see, she had it
on good authority, that
"it is all that is made."

Ridiculous? Indeed –
on the face of it. Yet,
in tacitly subscribing
to a proposition seemingly
so outrageous, wasn't she
anticipating – by those
selfsame seven centuries –
the cutting edge of
science?

And – it has to be said again –
she did have it on
the highest of all
authorities.

Being

Be content to
wait in the dark,
as the shepherds did –
to wait at the very
heart of your being,
with no attempt at
self-persuasion:
the experience will
carry its own conviction,
a sense of assurance
spreading through all of life –
even the problem areas
acquiring a kind of
validity, a wholeness
of meaning and purpose
of their own; and, pervading
all, a sense of given-ness – of
gift – to receive which
one need only – *can* only –
stretch out an open hand,
in a gesture of willingness
to receive.

And the gift? Ah – actually,
it's a *loss* – of all sense of
God "out there"; and
in its place the
awareness of
one's own life as
part of God's own
Being.

Bereavement Revisited

In vain my eyes have sought
the line of distant hills,
from whose very sight
I have drawn such comfort;
the horizon, too, dividing
what lies within my ken
from that which lies beyond:
the meeting place of Earth
and Heaven vanished,
overnight.
　　　　And in its place
a drab-grey sheet, stretching
from Heaven's infinitude
down to all that's left
of Mother Earth – a
lone tree outside my
house, doing its best
to reassure me that what
vanished overnight has
merely, for time being,
passed from sight.

Blank Cheque

Lord, I bring this day
to you, knowing that
it does not have to be
lived as every other day,
but – like a blank page
in my diary – left,
for *you* to fill.

Breakdown

Slowly fades the light,
as reason's sun sets,
and the darkness falls
in spirit's night.
The house is shut –
bolted, and barred –
and ghosts walk,
howling, along the
echoing corridors
of the mind.

And in a corner,
the spirit cringes,
conjuring up
fantasies of
all manner of devils
lurking just outside,
where – did it but know –
it is God who waits,
the door shut
in his face.

By No Means
Just Hot Air

Briefly, we had been
very close; yet –
even so –
we hadn't met:
a hot-air balloonist,
low enough to have
exchanged greetings
with me, had I been
in my garden, instead
of my armchair;
both of us risen early,
to exercise our faith
in that which is unseen:
to lift us above
the ordinary things
of life – mine
vested in the Spirit, his
simply in the buoyancy
provided by a mere
difference in density
between hot air
and cold.

He had entrusted his
very life to unseen
truth: could I – rising
to the occasion –
do the same?

Candle Power

Our lives are
the wick, embedded in
the wax – which is
God, from whom
we draw the energy
which fuels the flame
that enables us to be
a source of his Light
in the world.

Caritas?

Morning upon morning
they pour through my door,
as uninvited as a flash flood,
and equally unstoppable;
each envelope a sluice-gate which,
once opened, threatens to swamp
my feelings with its fundraiser-
honed, gift-backed appeal:
emotional blackmail,
standing charity
on its head.

    So it is that (standing
    on *my* head too, it seems)
    I find myself recycling – yes,
    recycling – charities…
    With rainforests much in mind
    (of which those envelopes and
    their voluminous contents
    were once a living part), and, no,
    not the little black boy, lacking
    the shelter that the umbrella
    they sent me was said to symbolize,
    I drop envelope upon envelope –
    unopened and unread – into the
    Green Bin, outside my door.

Outside my life now, too
(I kid myself), as I write out
cheques for the less-likely-
to-be-remembered ones: the
Prisoners of Conscience, and
Victims of Torture, Befrienders
of the Earth, and Womankind –
to say nothing of the
Deaf-blind, inhabiting their
unimaginable world.

    Blackmail –
    emotional or otherwise –
    parts people from their money, yes,
    but the outcome neither truly "gift",
    nor wholly "charitable".

Chance Encounter –
or was it?

I was sitting
by the roadside
of my life –
taking a breather,
so to say –
when he passed by.
No! – not like the priest
or the Levite: I could have
reached out and touched him –
just like that!

So – why didn't I?
Ah, you see –
he reached out
and touched me
first.

Christmas 2004

It's said,
of the elephant,
that it never forgets –
but what? I mean, *what*
does it "never forget"? –
one thing, I'm sure –
what it means to be
an elephant.

But Man?
Has he forgotten
what it means to
be a man – made
(as we're told)
in the image of
God? Strange,
it may seem, but
that doesn't mean
anything extra special –
like walking on water,
or turning it into wine.

'I come in the little things,'
says God, like enjoying
the sunshine – deep blue
in the distance, bright green
through the leaves – as one
shops for the simple necessities
of life, and enjoys the passing
company of one's
fellow human beings.
What place has
war – with its
"smart" weapons,
and daisy cutter bombs –
in such a setting?
How could one such,
about his business
of "just being human",
behead his fellow man in
cold blood, or, for that matter,
crucify him?

May then, this Christmas, of
Two Thousand Years and Four,
change all that, and more,
much more:
restore Man
to himself
again.

Christmas 2005

Christmas?
No – Christ-*mass!* –
but, alas, *"mass"* as in
mass spending sprees,
mass over-eating,
mass over-drinking,
with, everywhere,
a *mass* of fairy lights
and Christmas trees –
a *mass* of money
changing hands:
mass exploitation,
for commercial ends.

But –
it need not be always X-mas,
where X stands for
what we have long since
disregarded,
long since
forgot:
it can yet
be ***Christ-mass*** –
as we celebrate
the coming
of new Life,
new Love,
and new Being
into a world
that has lost
its way.

Christmas 2006

It's said that Christmas comes
but once a year, though nowadays –
as like as not – what comes is
more a mockery, a travesty
of all that Christmas ought to be.
Yet can we take heart! – for, truth is,
that the spirit of Christmas
comes to us, not once,
not twice, or even thrice! –
but, more times than are days
within the year.
It comes each time there is
new life, each time a baby's born;
it comes each time a life is saved,
each time a wound is healed –
each time a wrong is righted,
each time new love is sealed.
So! Let us celebrate
"all-the-year-round" Christmas,
and not just *one* day,
now flawed.

Christmas 2007

Roots,
long and deep,
find nourishment,
firm anchorage
as well; but,
surfacing,
in vain seek
sustenance,
strong stay
in storm.

So – Christmas:
roots long, strong,
and erstwhile deep,
riding the surface
now – questing
cheap cheer;
unmindful of those
fast-becoming-far-off
depths where, alone,
are its riches
found.

Christmas TV Commercial

'What do you want for Christmas?'
the TV programme said,
and showed us toys and pastimes,
and books to read in bed.

What do you want for Christmas?
A tree with fairy lights?
And cake with almond icing,
balloons, and party nights?

What do you want for Christmas?
fat turkey, stuffed and roast?
And then a glass of rich red wine —
is that what you want most?

       *   *   *

The housewife staggered homeward,
with parcels in her bag,
and parcels under both her arms;
her burdens made her sag.

'I'd loike to meet the man,' she said,
'who started all this Christmoos —
it's nowt but fuss and fret and fume,
for folks the loikes of oos.'

       *   *   *

Not 'What would you like for Christmas?',
but 'What are you ready to give?'
that's what the programme might have asked,
to make our Christmas live.

Then, for that Christmas present,
we each of us might say,
'I'd really *like* to meet the Man,
who started Christmas Day.'

(circa 1970)

Colour Bar

Black beetle, struggling,
legs aloft, frantically
thrashing the air, desperate
for someone to care enough
to turn you right way up,
and save you
from rotting
in the sun.

Merely to touch you
would sharp-shudder
me - yet will I attempt,
with my clumsy shoe,
to put you back on
your legs again, and
hope, thus, to avoid
too close a sight of
your repulsive self.

Are you that ugly?
Or did I – seeing in you
my own dark self – recoil
from the shadow within?

Had I but known! Gladly
would I have bent –
knees to the ground –
to turn my dark side
right way up, and
greet him as
a friend.

Common Things

The warming sun
brings belated buds
to blossom, as the sound
of sawn wood, and of
spade cleaving the
cloddy ground mingle with
the mesmeric murmur
of bees, out on their round.
Yet does it fail to shatter
the all-pervading sense
of peace:

over the hedge wafts
the strange sweet smell
of fresh-mown grass,
provoking God knows
what memories and
meanings from the past —
of schoolboy cricket,
teenage tennis,
mixed doubles on a
summer's eve, and
picnics with the children
on the lawn — the ghosts
of yesterday haunting
the ghost within; ghost
haunting ghost with
visions of life as it was,
these long years since,
intimations of normality
breaking the staling crust
of middling age, to renew
the deep awareness of
the uncommonness of
common things.

(circa mid-1960s)

Computer-Wise

The accomplishments of
my computer are many,
and often enviable,
one, head and shoulders
above the rest:
the ability to "undo"
a full hundred of its
most recent actions,
be they "unforced errors"
(as the sportsmen say), or
clearly culpable mistakes.

Could but we mere mortals
do the same – from a
single word, so obviously
out of place, to an
innocent phrase, even so,
misunderstood; from a
veritable verbal torrent,
deep-felt, but ill-conceived,
and causing grave offence, to
that "Yes" (or "No") which
we convince ourselves to be
not quite a lie, and yet
intended to deceive;
and, worst of all, the
angry outburst – in
"bold",
and *italics,* and
even **_underlined_** –
whereby, in moments,
is love's labour
of a lifetime
lost:
could we
but click on "Edit",
and then – in Life's
drop-down menu –
on "Undo"…

Confessional

Must I come again, simply to say
what I have said twice, thrice – no,
more – full dozen times before?

    Is there no other way to treat
    of the treachery that ever lurks,
    and ever will, it seems, within
    the bulwarks of my rebel heart;
    no other way, save to rehearse it all
    afresh, though it be the same sad,
    sick catalogue of yore?

Is it – can it be – that I yet
crucify you anew, with each day's
crop of fresh betrayals, pin you
to the bare, brute wood of
another cross, which, as well,
I have helped hew? And must I –
must I – crucify, not only you,
but me? Is there
no other way?

    Then –
    so let it be.
    And, stretched,
    guilt-laden, on my cross,
    I shall address myself to you,
    all innocent, on yours: confess
    aloud, in the painful presence
    of my brother man, what would
    have been so easy – oh, *so* easy –
    to have kept within the confines
    of my own heart – 'twixt
    you and me
    alone.

Contemplation – and After

I sat, quiet as a
mouse, still as a
watchful squirrel –
motionless as a
bird on a chimney
pot, or a
weathervane,
undisturbed by
even the breath
of a breeze.

But –
as I rose again,
it was to remember
that life is movement,
and – like a dance –
grave or gay,
swift or slow,
temperate or
tempestuous
in turn; calm,
or white water,
as it flows from
the source of
all Being.

---------- Conversation Piece ----------

'Just think
of nothing –
nothing at all.
No! Don't just
not think of *anything* –
think of *nothing:*
just try to envisage
nothing existing.'

'But that's impossible.
How can nothing *exist?*
Do you mean just
empty space?'

'Well – what then, of space?
Does *it* exist? If so,
you're not thinking of
nothing when you're
thinking of space, but of
something that's
infinitely big!'

'It's endless, isn't it? –
I mean, this line of thought:
it's just playing with words,
and going round in circles.'

'No! For does it not show
that existence *itself*
is set in the heart of
a mystery extending
infinitely, in each and all of
Einstein's four dimensions?
Yet, still, do we take it for granted –
from the meanest flower
that blows, to the nature, and
being, of our very selves.
Ponder – daily, hourly, and
moment by every precious
moment – the mystery,
majesty, beauty, and –
yes – *holiness* of an
infinitude of Universe
that sustains Life
on one tiny speck of it
we call Planet Earth.
There would be no place then
in Einstein's time-and-space
for inhumanity
of man, to man,
or strife – or
bloody wars.'

'You mean, we'll get
this human life of ours
into perspective
(*and* act accordingly)
only when we view it
against this backdrop
of Infinity?'

'Putting the Universe
into a nutshell –
yes.'

Convertible Currency

Suffering is like going on a journey
you neither expected, nor chose to make –
like finding yourself on the wrong train,
a long-distance one, at that; and, moreover
(for reasons best known to the authorities),
there's no communication cord for you to pull:
in fact, you're committed to going all the way.

Not having planned to make such a journey,
you lack most things you'll need –
and frantically search your pockets,
hoping to find the wherewithal
to buy yourself out of the pain:
bribe the guard to stop the train –
or whatever –
but, to no avail.
In fact, you're virtually broke,
and in no position to help yourself
or anyone else.
But –
even so –
you manage to see the journey through,
and, at last, you're free to go.

Alone, and in unfamiliar territory,
you cautiously take an exploratory walk,
looking, with fresh eyes, on what yet seem
familiar sights –
hearing familiar sounds, too,
despite the unusual language
people seem to be talking.
(It's almost like "speaking in tongues").

You notice a woman then –
she's sitting alone,
and quietly weeping,
but somehow you know
(but you don't know how)
that it's not in sorrow
nor in pain,
but, simply for
the joy of things.

You pluck up courage
to go and sit by her.
and – big surprise –
she addresses you
in words you understand.
'So you made the journey, too?'

'Yes – but really through no choice of mine.'

'That's almost always so,' she says, 'and you
think you're destitute now – penniless, in fact.
I did, too, until I looked in my purse.
Have you looked in your pockets?',
she queries then – but as casually as maybe.
'No point,' I say, 'I turned them inside out
long before I got off the train.'
'Ah – yes,' she responds, thoughtfully now,
'but, if I were you, I'd look again.'

There's something about the way she says it,
that brooks no more debate,
no more delay.
So –
though it's with little hope of success –
I delve into my trouser pockets,
to find them simply *loaded* with coins,
but, of a currency I'd never seen before.

Sensing my bewilderment, she speaks again –
this time with a kind of holy glee.
'It's yours,' she says, 'you see, the coins
are *tokens* – tokens of the suffering
you've endured – privately, you may think,
but actually, if rightly borne, it's
on behalf of all humanity.
Spent, so to say, in loving concern,
on a fellow human being,
they can enable your suffering to
curtail what remains of his, and
bring it to an earlier end.

'You find that impossible to believe?
"It would have to be a miracle?" you say.
Well, I suppose, it *is* a *kind* of miracle.
And – remember! – those thus healed,
find *their* pockets, too, are filled.
Aren't you glad, now,
you travelled the distance
on that train?'

She gets up.
'Excuse me –
I'm off to spend some more now.
The thing is' (and this, her
parting shot) – 'the more you spend
of this kind of money, the more
you find you've got.
That's the difference
between worldly wealth,
and the wealth
that suffering
can bring.'

And in that moment
she was gone, but
I hadn't noticed
any sign of wings.

Counterpoint

'That knee,' I muttered,
a little tetchily, as I was
getting out of bed, 'that *knee*
spells trouble for me today.'

> *(My feet had hardly reached the floor,*
> *when there was an almighty roar.*
> *No, I wasn't the cause of it – it was*
> *five thousand miles away:*
> *a stray landmine had blown off*
> *both feet, of a farmer in Angola.)*

My breakfast was ready and waiting
(I prepare it overnight – you see –
it means a less *bothersome* start
to the day): knife, fork, and spoon
laid out on the table, the cereal
ready and waiting, in a bowl.
'The same old thing gets *boring*,
when you have it every day –
it would be nice to have a change,'
I thought, as I drowned it
in full-cream milk.

> *(It was at that very moment*
> *that a young woman – a Sudanese –*
> *was offering her new-born son such milk*
> *as she had left, in her near-empty*
> *breast: a few gulps, and it was gone –*
> *it was just as I took the first*
> *mouthful of Pecan and Maple*
> *Crunch.)*

A shower, then – to wash away
the cobwebs, so to say, and launch me
on what the weather man was promising
to be another fine, warm, but not too torrid
day – 'just temperate', I'd heard him say.

> *(But I'd hardly got round to*
> *drying myself when that self-same*
> *Sudanese, her baby on her back now –*
> *the temperature well above blood heat –*
> *was setting out on a five-mile trek for*
> *water, a ten-litre jar miraculously*
> *balanced on her head: the only showers*
> *she was interested in, were six months*
> *overdue.)*

Armed with a lengthy shopping list,
I pushed my trolley up and down
the Supermarket aisles – the shelves
stacked high with all that I could ever
want – and more: from ready meals
to "super" deals ("two for the price of one"),
from two-litre bottles of full-cream milk,
to blockbusters filled with "pure spring water",
flown in (at what price?) from far-off
mountain range.

> *(By the time I was through the checkout,*
> *and had asked for ten pounds "cash back",*
> *the Sudanese woman had been raped,*
> *and – with her baby – left to die.)*

After lunch, and what I considered
a well-earned rest (you know – feet up,
and, if you're lucky, a nap) perchance
to dream; but, in the event, a
middle-of-the-day nightmare,
from which (I have to confess) I was
more than glad to waken.

> *(In Afghanistan, there was a man*
> *who was also suffering nightmares, but –*
> *unlike me –kept wide awake,*
> *by regular electric shocks,*
> *and they certainly weren't*
> *to his head.)*

My evening was a restful one
(my knee surviving what - you must
agree - had been quite a *trying* day
for me); so, with no sensational
news on the box, I opted
for an early night: an
uneventful ending to an
uneventful day.

> *(But whilst I was offering up my*
> *prayers, what I didn't know, in fact,*
> *was that there were* two *of us just then,*
> *praying to the self-same God it seems –*
> *one difference, though (of many):*
> *that* I *was hoping – praying, indeed –*
> *that I would see another day, but* he*?*
> *⬜uite otherwise: he blew himself up*
> *with thirty-nine others,*
> *just as I was climbing*
> *into bed.)*

And, whilst I slept, God wept
for his Creation.

Decision Time

It is as if
we were simply
keeping ourselves warm by
sharing the comforts and
the camaraderie of a
camp fire, throwing on
another log when
the flames threaten
to die down – fearing
lest we lose sight of
our fellow humans' faces,
shown up, fitfully, in the
light of the flickering flames;
all about us, the ill-lit
environs of our earthly life,
and beyond, the deep
darkness of the unknown –
extending into the
unknowable: the
infinitudes
of space.

'□uick! – another log!' we say –
as we start to shiver at
the very thought of being
on our own: alone at the
epicentre of a mystery
of incomprehensible
dimensions, and of a
significance beyond
human wit ever to
understand.

So, what about a song, to
keep our spirits up? Or even
another war? – *that* should
keep our minds off the
ultimates of our existence,
hopefully for a whole
decade, and
more.

But –
what about
quitting the camp fire,
and venturing into
the Night, through which
alone, can we reach
the Light.
i

Deep Breathing

Breathe in God's
hope – breathe out
despair; breathe in his
peace – and banish
fear. Breathe in his
joy, and transform
pain; his healing,
and dispel dis-ease.

But –
breathe in his Grace,
and glimpse the
very features
of his face!

Despair Dispelled

I'd handed in my
membership card of
the human race,
and was scraping
along the bottom,
in desperate need
of the wherewithal
to pump the water
from my hold,
and re-float me
on the sea
of life.

But, it wasn't a
pump that rescued me –
just a phone call
from a fellow
human being,
in need of my help;
and, in the instant,
I had surfaced, and
was on my way
again.

Destination... ?

It came to me the other day,
that I'd travelled a hundred miles
to cut myself a slice of bread –
and a thousand miles to toast it,
and several thousand more to
spread the butter and marmalade –
and goodness knows how many
thousands more to eat it: and
that's just travelling round the Sun
at eighteen miles a second, and
taking no account, what's more,
of Sun's circling of the Galaxy.

  We're spacemen all
  (women and children, too),
  hurtling along
  on spaceship "Earth";
  but here's the rub —
  to *where?*

So – why not let
the toast burn
for once, and give
quality time to
the answer?

Differing to Agree

It was Martha,
to Mary:
'I wish you'd come and
help, there's so much
I've got to do.'

'I, too.'

'What, you?'

'Yes,
I too,'
said Mary,
hands resting,
clasped,
upon her lap.

'What can you do,
hands clasped,
like that?'

'I pray.

'And so,
dear sister,
though we differ,
yet do we agree:

'Or clasped or free,
work needs be found
for hands to do –
thus, though 'tis true,
we differ,
yet,
more so,
do we agree.'

Digging Up The Past

My mood
was one of doubt,
unconvinced as I was
of a significant find,
or even of its being
the right time or place
to start. As well, I feared
what I might uncover
by way of rubbish from the
past – tempted to leave well
alone: I had climbed far –
why add to the rigours
of the climb the labour of
an archaeological dig?
Why not just enjoy the view
from where I was? But the
climb had been tough – even
thus far – burdened, as I was,
with the wherewithal to dig:
why quit now?

> So – I made a tentative
> beginning, soon taking heart
> to find that the deeper I dug,
> the easier it seemed to become.
> And, forsaking my clumsy tools
> lest they should damage
> what – perchance – lay buried
> there, I gently scooped away the
> remaining soil – soft and yielding
> now – with cupped hands,
> clasped, as might have been,
> in prayer.

Perhaps they were.
For – in truth – I found,
laid bare, not just my
buried past, but the
present, from which –
so often – I had sought to
flee, unaware that it is
there, and there alone, that
life is truly lived: in the
Nowness – wherein lies,
as well, the Eternity of
ordinary things.

Dimensions

Time was,
when we were
satisfied
with just three
common or
garden ones:
forward and
back, up and
down, and from
one side to
the other.

Time came, then (in
Einstein's understanding),
to be, itself, a fourth –
in some ways
common sense:
each occupying
his or her own place
in the to and fro,
from side to side,
and the ups and downs
of life – with all this
at a point in time,
designated as
"historical".

Then –
and, as it were,
in time's fullness –
the physicist added
to Einstein's four
six more, to make
full ten, with a possible
eleventh (and, who knows? –
even more, up to
an unknown "n-th");
and all this to satisfy
the demands of
pure mathematics.

But, what if,
despite such
cerebration, it was
an 'n plus *one*-th'
that finally revealed
the significance
(or otherwise)
of all those
extra ones? –
the dimension of
un-knowing.

(The last line is a reference to the "The Cloud of Unknowing", by a 14th century mystic.)

Easter - on Easy Terms

Hot cross buns
in packets of six;
"Three for the price of
two" the label said.
Yes – eighteen crosses
for the price of twelve:
what a bargain, indeed,
it was…

   There were mere
   three, on that
   first of all
   Good Fridays,
   but of wood –
   rough-hewn –
   a dying man
   on each:

how much easier to
contemplate the ones
of striped dough, and
pristine white! – on
soft brown buns,
all eighteen, laced
with aromatic spices,
toasted and buttered,
and running
in jam, not
blood.

First Light

My favourite armchair
(appropriately enough
an "orthopaedic" one)
demands – even dictates –
good posture, as one accepts
its firm embrace.

   Straight-backed, and with
   padded, horizontal wooden
   arms, it offers firm anchorage
   for elbow joints – enabling
   forearms, wrists, hands, and even
   fingers to say words like "Yes,"
   and "No," "Come,", and "Go,"
   with unanticipated eloquence.
   Even one word, spoken so,
   can (like a picture) be worth a
   thousand, vocalised.

And this chair is
where I spend much time,
contemplating God, and the
ultimates of life and death,
the infinitudes of space, and
the doubtful future of the
tiny speck in it we know as
Planet Earth.

   With elbows firmly planted on
   those orthopaedic arms, forearms
   slanted outwards and upwards,
   palms open, and fingers aimed
   heavenwards, I am able to say –
   no – *shout,* "YES!" to the whole
   panoply of joy and sorrow,
   hope and despair, peace
   and pandemonium,
   love (and lack of it) that
   makes up this human life
   of ours, and yet leave –
   inviolate –
   the silence of
   first light.

First Things First

I prayed for sleep, but
sleep stayed away.
I prayed for peace – the
peace which is "beyond
all human understanding",
and sleep came to stay.

Gardeners' Question Time
(23.11.03)

The chairman (tongue in cheek, it's true)
spoke of 'sitting with our feet up,
encroaching on the vital business of
Christmas shopping – talking gardening,'
he said, 'when all you really want is to
do further damage to your Credit Card:
continue your battle with the tidal waves of
jolly shoppers, buying all those sorts of things
you wouldn't touch with a barge pole
for eleven months of the year.'

   It was too near the bone for comfort;
   and I winced despondently as I
   admitted to myself that it would be
   true of most who would have heard
   his sad surmise.

How is it that we get so much so
wrong? – turn "-less" to "-ish" in
"selflessness", make mockery of
Love Incarnate – *incarcerate*
instead; sometimes the truth
too near at hand to see that love
makes no demand on Credit Cards;
nor does one need join jostling
crowds to find it – less still have
dealings with unpalatable things.

   It's simply *there!* – 'twixt you
   and me, and her and him; and
   rooted deep, in the stranger
   at our door.

God's Alchemy
- Further Thoughts on Bereavement -

Consumed still, as I am,
by such sense of loss
and pain – yet, do I
believe that time will be
when pain becomes
transformed into
a kind of holy joy,
and loss into
mysterious
gain.

God's Atoms

Neutron-sundered
nuclei, chain-reacting
with their neighbours,
vindicate Einstein, and
convert a handful
of matter into a
city-scything
flesh-searing,
man-melting
fireball, paling
the midday sun.

Suspicion-split,
fear-fused, they rear
their mushroom heads
to high heaven: fungi
growing on a hot-bed of
hatred, in the cellars
of men's minds.

A-bombs or H-bombs,
they are yet God's atoms,
fission or fusion, still
his power, perverted
by Man's continued
failure to take his brother
by the hand.

Thus God's great blessing,
atom-locked, and
burgled out of time,
must, under God,
yield true increase,
or man-mismanaged,
gene-mutate his future
to a nothingness of
lunacy, gaped out in
deserts, sterilized by
atom's rays that
might have served
God's ends.

(circa mid-1950s)

------------ **Grace** ------------

Words work through
meaning – shallow or
deep, edifying or
cheap – all but
self-evident in some,
others requiring the
services of a dictionary,
even an encyclopaedia,
to elucidate their full
import.

There are words, though,
which have no roots deep-
buried in the past, their very
sound synonymous with sense,
like "clip-clop", "hiss", "buzz",
"bang" and "plop".

Ironically – perversely, even –
they are categorized by a
word, six-syllabled, no less,
and one whose meaning, on the
face of it, could be hardly more
opaque: "*onomatopœic*",
for goodness sake!

And, yes, for Goodness' sake are
other words – most precious these,
of all – their etymological pedigree
impeccable; and, far from
onomatopœic, they yet
speak to us most plainly
through the beauty of
their sound.

Of such words is "grace" –
many-faceted, it's true, from
His Grace the Duke of Wherever,
to a prayer of thanks for food;
from extra time to pay a debt,
to a humbleness of mood,
and even "grace" of movement
which is effortless
and smooth.

But, it is as an attribute of
God that the word bursts
bud, and blossoms
like the rose.

To say that God is
"gracious" is to take but
one small, stumbling step
towards an understanding of
what it means to speak –
often all too glibly – of
"the grace of God".
It is as though meaning
takes on such richness –
such fullness – that it
overflows into the very
sound itself.

Monosyllabic, and
mere five letters long,
it speaks of love without limit,
and love that sets no bound –
a love that comes to meet us,
greet us, whilst we are yet
a great way off. There is
forgiveness, too, implicit
in this wondrous,
five-lettered,
monosyllabic
sound –
forgiveness that
states no conditions,
save one:
our readiness,
our willingness,
to accept.

Such love, and
such forgiveness,
are like the two halves
of a critical mass of
pure Goodness, which,
coming together in the
soul, generate – with
explosive joy – new
life, new
love, new
being.

Heavenly Horticulture:

My life is, as it were, a plant
rooted in You, and growing
in Your truth, budding
in Your knowledge, and
flowering in Your love.

Help from an Unexpected Quarter

My computer is helping me
to pray.
Surprised?
Yes – so was I.

Of course, it has
innumerable drop-down
menus dedicated to
solving particular
problems (God has,
too).

But there's something else
my computer claims to do:
it *"enables"!* – telling me
that (among other things)
it has "enabled" my
anti-virus software,
so that it can perform
its allotted tasks.

In the past,
I have asked
for God to
help me
(i.e. for one of those
drop-down menus
to appear); but now
(and much more
comprehensively)
I'm beginning to pray
simply to be
"enabled".

And that covers
everything.

---------- Holy Communion ----------

Scruffy-looking,
squatting on the
pavement outside the
Supermarket doors,
looking at me
reproachfully –
reduced, as he
is, to merely
watching the
world go by:
a world of which,
so little time ago,
he had rejoiced
to be a part;

I keep my distance –
walking past – there's
no way in which I'm
getting involved.

Haunting me now,
that look – driving me
to return, to give voice to
my concern, still keeping
my distance though; and he,
having every reason for
doing so, disdaining my
easy-spoke condolences:
my kindness-on-demand.

Into the Supermarket – its
bright lights and refrigerated
racks, row on row, loaded
with tempting snacks. A whiff of
conscience then – seeing,
in mind's eye, his eyes light up
in response to even *one* item
from those tempting shelves, as
I imagine taking it back to share
with him: a sort of impromptu
holy communion, between
the two of us.

What's that I'm saying?
Communion? –
between *me* and a
light-brown mongrel
dog? – a dumb animal,
tethered to a drain-pipe,
anxiously awaiting his
master's return…

Did I say *"dumb"*?
But what of those eyes –
that *look* of anxious love
and fear that his master,
for all that, might *never*
come? Wasn't *that*
communion? –

and holy,
too.

I. T.

Far,
and long,
have we travelled,
to make knowledge
so easy to convey –
even the knowledge
of how it is conveyed
voluminous enough
to justify at least
a Bachelor's Degree:

    "the wireless" first,
    then "television", (each image
    "worth a thousand words");
    and, bursting late upon the
    scene, the "personal computer",
    with "word processor", and
    "databases" accessed at
    button's touch – the whole of
    the Encyclopaedia Britannica
    on a single "CD - ROM".
    And – latest of all – "emailing",
    with "surfing the Worldwide Web" –
    and "Google" the Open Sesame
    to a Global Knowledge Store.

So –
what more?

    Midst such welter of
    technology, have we, in fact,
    forgotten the simplest (but
    most profound) technique
    of all, whereby is acquired
    the deepest of all
    knowledge? –

    "Be *still* –
    and know
    that I am
    God."

In a City Church

For this deep calm
in a raging sea
of sound;
for this oasis
of silence
in a city
desert,
I thank you, Lord.

Vaulted stones
do not contain
you, retain you
for their own;
yet is it easier
for the spirit's
outreach –
questing –
to breach the
barricades
of self,
and find you here,
anew; though –
quintessentially –
do you yet dwell
in the very
heart of
Man.

In-sight

You see, there's
this life "of mine"
(as I'm wont to think of it) −
a "city", if you like,
of which I've been given
the "freedom", to live in it
as I will; or seeing it
for what it really is:
"my" life, but part
of God's own Being;
and, with that selfsame
free will, choosing
to let *him* live it
with me, and on
my behalf − and
my true state of
 being.

----------- **Intimations of Mortality** ------------

There were more passengers than seats;
and, in a defining moment, when a woman –
young and pretty, and with kindly, smiling face –
stood, and offered me her place, I knew that
she, at least, had deemed me old, and I
accepted, with good grace.

                    *   *   *

Assiduously, I went about my road drill at the
kerb: "Look right, look left, look right again."
That's it! All clear! Let's go!

'Hey! Wait!' she said – quite elderly herself,
I thought – intentions naught but good;
my drill, alas, misunderstood.
'It's true, you know, we're long time dead!
I'll see you to the other side,' (of Jordan,
might it be, she spoke?); my body
safe across the road, but –
how hurt my pride!

                    *   *   *

I stood, for a moment companionless –
the party at its height. Across the swirling sea
of faces, a bright young thing – my daughter's
friend – had spotted me, and plunging in,
awash with words: 'My! What surprise is *this!*
How *nice!* You *are* up late! And not too tired?'
And, with no more ado, she kissed me –
no! – not on *cheek,* but smack on *lips!*
Well – after all – I mean to say! –
It was *quite* safe – there *are* no hormones
in old age ‒ no danger then, that I'd mistake
her free-and-easy ways for bold-as-brass
coquetry (or worse).

                    *   *   *

I'd jotted down a few coherent sentences
(it was, in fact, a poem); and, in a rash moment,
thought to share them with my daughter's
(selfsame) friend – the party long since over,
and my ruffled feathers smoothed.

'That's *good!* That's very, *very* good,'
she said, as she eyed me up and down
(she refrained from patting me on the head,
as most certainly she would have done,
had I been eight, not eighty). And her look?
It had so plainly said, 'I wouldn't have thought
you had it in you! Well – I mean –
not at *your* age!' I forestalled her:
'Perhaps I had to reach this age
to have such thoughts at all...'

* * *

'Do be careful! Wrap up well! And,
what*ever* you do, don't *overdo* it!'

But – the choice is stark indeed:
to sit, be-slippered, in an easy chair –
to vegetate, sans teeth, sans eyes,
sans taste, sans everything, awaiting
the Grim Reaper's solemn offices
to end it all "as sound and fury,
signifying nothing" – or,
throwing caution to the winds,
allow oneself to think new
thoughts, to dream new
dreams, and replenish
the Spirit at the
Wellspring of
all Being.

Joy

Joy is no joy, which
needs to state its terms,
and so deny its own true nature –
which of such substance is,
that neither time,
nor chance,
nor circumstance
erodes,
or ever can.

Letter to "The Lancet"

In times of contemplation
I let my hands lie open
in my lap, palms turned
upward – the gesture
one of waiting, and
expectancy.

Now, as well,
at night, I find
tranquillity in
lying, hands open
once again, palms
upward – in Childlike
anticipation of the
gift of sleep. It's
more effective than
Temazepam.

Litter -
- Ruminations on a Word -

How is it that a single word
should have to bear the weight
of such diversity of meaning?
What quirk of semantics
has brought that about?

Commonly, it conjures up
an image (as the dictionary
has it) of "rubbish, such as
paper, food, or bottles, left
lying in the open, or a
public place". It might well
have added, "old cookers,
washing machines, fridges
and beds, dumped at
beauty spots."

The word salvages at least
some respectability as
"the bed straw of a stabled
beast", whilst, as "a means
of transporting the sick",
it comes near to being
sanctified (remember the
paralytic, lowered through
the roof to the feet of
Christ?). Alas, from the
sublime to the ridiculous –
and worse: "a granular material
for the indoor use of cats...".

What, then, of the meaning
in its most common use?
Strange though it be,
a *modicum* of untidiness
makes home homely –
the view too, from your
favourite vantage point as
beautiful as it ever was,
despite the clapped-out
cooker at your feet.
But – replace the cooker
with autumn leaves littered,
yes, *littered,* ankle-deep – what then?
(Perhaps the lexicologist would have
served us better with "man-made,
obtrusive, and out of place.")

And what of the one who
put the cooker there? – or
threw the Coca Cola bottle
over my garden fence? –
to say nothing of the countless
millions who daily disgorge their
chewing-gum onto the pavements
of our city streets. Whence springs
the indignation that tempts me
to consider them no longer part
of the human race? Is it the crass
indifference shown towards the
feelings of their fellow men? And –
more so – the sheer contempt for
the beauty of our planet?

Indifference, and contempt,
enter the mind by the back door,
to deaden it, insidiously, as by
a drug. What matter, then, if we
save the planet from destruction by
an atom bomb, but lose, meanwhile,
the ability to appreciate its wonder
and its beauty; and, likewise,
all consideration for
our fellow man?

Lost, and Found

My life was broken into
pieces, and I was lost –
that is, until I found
the pieces fitting together
into a brand-new shape.

Making Music

Let scientist dissect this
symphony of sound, evoked by
men, full hundred, from instruments,
cunningly devised, long since, by
those who, knowing nought of science,
yet had the instinct and intuition to
fashion from prime matter –
wood, skin, hair, and shining metal –
these mouthpieces of heaven.

Let him transcribe them
into waveforms – display, and
analyse them as spectral distributions,
in the only language that he knows;
as well, let him dispense with such
archaic crudities as violins, and flute's
elusive voice, and substitute mere
sinusoidal oscillations – fundamental
with harmonics mixed – match
note for note, and tone for tone,
these relics of the past.
Might it not be argued
that in such terms lies
deeper understanding
of the composer's art?

Yet would it lack
the one ingredient needful to
add Eternity to music's voice –
for music needs men to make it.
And let it be with horse hair
given bite by dried sap,
drawn across twisted
sheep's gut with the touch
of God; with pursed lips, too,
coaxing, God knows how, from
flute and flageolet, from
trumpet and trombone,
the soft sibilants of woodwind
and triumphal tones of brass;
men who, agonized by the notes
before them, suffer the pangs
of childbirth to create anew
the masterpiece,
each time they play.

This is the fashion in which
music is ever made, and
ever will be – by men who,
having heard the voice of God,
cannot keep silence.

(This poem was written in 1961, whilst flying back from Vienna, where I had spent a fortnight as a consultant, at the International Atomic Energy Agency. I had worked hard, and played hard as well – going to several concerts at the Musikverein, a wonderful experience, out of which this poem was born. It was complete by the time I had landed at Heathrow, late, one winter's night.)

Maundy Thursday

Reading it, it seemed
so simple – 'Just say,
"Now I come to Thee," '
and (it implied) all
shall be well, and
all manner of thing
shall be well.

   But my voice
   was too weak,
   and too husky
   to speak.

And then it was that I
(as it were) heard You
spelling it out for me:
'Come unto me,' You said,
and I will give you rest.
Let not your heart
be troubled,
neither let it
be afraid.'

   But I couldn't believe
   what I'd heard,
   and was still unable
   to utter a word.

Yet am I coming, Lord –
and *have* been
(as best I could)
as I've journeyed through
the Lenten weeks –
to keep my tryst
with You:

yes – tomorrow – from
twelve o'clock
till three.

More Than You Anticipated...

'Please hang up
and try again,'
the phone had said
repeatedly.
And I fell to
wondering what
such words would
signify, if God had
spoken them to me:

'Relax, let go, and
desist from fruitless
expectations. But
don't give up, just
bide your time,
and you'll find that,
after all, there *is* an
answer forthcoming,
from the other end –

but perhaps not
the one you were
expecting.'

Morning Prayer

Your Strength for my body,
through the day,
Your Peace for my mind,
along Life's way;
Your Joy in my spirit
ever to stay.

New Year Resolution:

to treat each year
as if it were a lifetime,
each month as if it were
a year; each week as
month, each hour as week,
each fleeting minute like an
hour – each moment
an Eternal Now.

This poem was written during a bout of near-despair, following my wife's first stroke.

Nil Desperandum

I will not let Thee go,
except Thou bless me –
not in the beatific moment
in an armchair, with slippered feet
beside a flickering fire, and
treasured tome, with problems
on the implications of the Trinity
nicely posited for simple cerebration
within the safety of an Ivory Tower –
but *here,* in the heat and heart
of battle, where the issue of the
soul's survival hangs as on a
single tortured thread, and
Hell's abyss – no longer a mere
theological concept awaiting
further cogitation on some other
cosy afternoon – gapes greedily
at the feet. With all defences down,
I cannot – dare not – let Thee go,
except Thou bless me.

Nothing Excluded

Each morning
I make bold
to throw wide
the doors of
my awareness
to an ever-present
and indwelling
guest, the Spirit of
Eternal Being:
permeating all,
from the smallest sub-
atomic particle in
my little finger
to the most distant
of the galaxies;
experiencing,
with me,
the tiniest details
of my day, down to
a single
heart beat – and,
yes – missed beats
and all.

(This narrative poem was set to music in 1999 as a Cantata for solo tenor, chorus, and string quartet (or organ).
It is, of course, based on the text of Chapter 9, in the Gospel of St John.)

Now Can I See!

You speak of trees –
I know not what they are,
save that they are strong enough
to bear my weight,
and tall.

You speak of flowers,
many-hued;
I know not
even what a colour be,
yet sweet enough
the fragrance of a rose,
to 'suage my sorrows,
all.

You speak of birds,
high-soaring,
on the insubstantial air;
such matter can I bare conceive –
yet do I know the beauty
of the blackbird's
call.

You speak of eyes,
with which you say
you see these things;
I know not even what it means
to see;
yet do I understand
the touch of lover's hand,
when – on mine –
it doth gently
fall.

* * *

A man there was,
who all but passed me by;
yet I, though sightless,
knew this man to be
strong like a tree,
his spirit, soaring
on the winds of heaven,
fragrant as a rose.

He spoke in riddles
that made instant sense:
of day, and night,
(though they are both the same to me) –
the day for work
(his father's work, he said),
the night that needs must idle be.

He spoke of light,
and I, who knows not sight,
nor light by which you sighted ones
do see,

yet understand
full well
his claim
to be the Light
that lighteneth the world.
Even my blindness
was, he said,
not loss,
but opportunity.

Strangely, then,
he spat upon the ground –
made clay,
and daubed it on my eyes.
'Go, wash in Siloam's Pool,'
was all he said.
I thought at first
how pointless
that it all did seem:
spittle, clay, and stagnant water.
yet came just then,
within my eyes,
a sense of warmth,
a glowing red,
that I as yet
knew not as light.
I simply washed away
the clay,
and found that I had sight!

* * *

The neighbours argued much
among themselves.
'Is not this the one
who sat and begged?' –
some saying,
'It is he,'
and others,
'Not so, this man can see.'
I said, simply,
'It *is* me.'

'How came this so?'
they asked me then,
and, disbelieving,
hauled me up
before the Pharisees,
who said, 'The man can but a sinner be,
since it was on the Sabbath Day
he healed the beggar's eyes with clay –
how can he be from God?'

They called my parents then,
and asked,
'Is this your son, born blind?
How is it that he now can see?'
But fearing it to be a trap,
they said,
I was indeed their son, born blind,
but argued that they knew not how
I now could see.
'Ask him,' they said, 'he is of age.'
And so they called me yet again –
demanded then,
'Give God the praise,
this man you say restored your sight,
but common sinner is.'

The time had come
to make my stand.
'Whether or not a sinner, he,
one thing I know,
that whereas was I sightless,
now can I see!'

They asked me yet again
what he had done –
how opened he mine eyes.
'Already have I told you!'
Then, angered, did I say,
'Wherefore? Would you then follow
in his way?'
They called me names,
and swore at me -
'You it is who follows him –
we follow none but Moses.'

Then did I let my fury fly!
'Well here's a marvellous thing! –
you know not whence he came,
yet he it was
who op'd my eyes!
Were this man not of God a son,
then naught could he have done!'

'Were you not altogether
born in sin? – yet would teach *us,*
who know and keep the Law
entire.
We cast you out –
excommunicate
you are!'

       * * *

Jesus was his name –
the man who gave me sight –
he got to know what they had done,
and sought me out,
and asked me plain,
did I believe
God had a son?
I answered thus,
'Who is he, Lord,
that I may then believe?'

Till dying day,
I'll ne'er forget
what next he said:
'With eyes that see now,
you have seen! –
'tis *I* – who speaks to thee.'

Somehow I'd known it all along –
he spoke with such authority,
as could from God alone have come.

I worshipped him.

Then to the Pharisees he said,
'Though came I that the blind might see,
yet might the sighted, blinded be.'

Then queried, did some Pharisees,
'Are we then blind?'

Jesus – whose words had fallen
on their ears in vain –
thus, sorrowing, replied:
'Though blind, you claim that yet you see,
and so your sin remains.'

* * *

So! now I see
how tall the tree –
how red the fragrant rose,
and catch the light
of love
in eye
of her
who loveth me!

The beginning and end of the previous poem comprise a poem within a poem –
with a simple change of tense:

Now Can I See (2)

You spoke of trees –
I knew not what they were,
save that they were strong enough
to bear my weight –
and tall.

    You spoke of flowers,
    many-hued:
    I knew not
    even what a colour was,
    yet sweet enough
    the fragrance of a rose,
    to 'suage my sorrows,
    all.

You spoke of birds,
high-soaring,
on the insubstantial air;
such matter could I bare conceive –
yet did I know the beauty
of the blackbird's
call.

    You spoke of eyes,
    with which you say
    you saw these things;
    I knew not even what it meant
    to see,
    yet did I understand
    the touch of lover's hand,
    when, on mine,
    it did gently
    fall.

But now I see
how tall the tree! –
how red the fragrant rose!
and catch the light
of love in eye
of her who
loveth me!

---------- On the Box ----------

From the comfort
of an armchair,
we view the news
as though through the
plate-glass window
of a shop: the choice is
ours! – to buy the goods or,
at the touch of a button,
move on to other "shops"
(we call them "channels")
where what's on offer is
more to our taste.

'All the world's a stage,'
said the Bard, but could
even he foresee
such theatre as this? –
where, from an armchair,
we can watch the players,
in a deadly game of war,
jostling for prime place
in the headlines with
the perpetrators of
serial murder,
gang rape, and
genocide.

Alas,
familiarity
breeds, if not contempt, then
indifference: how, otherwise,
could we so nonchalantly
shop around for more
palatable goods –
treat events, soul-shaking,
and epoch-making,
with such breath-taking
unconcern?

Indifferent, yes, but
satiate, too; we need
cast off familiarity's
cloak, and see News
new – not just *new*
news, but "old" news,
too:

"Today we interrupt our
programmes to bring you
graphic pictures – live – of
a crucifixion taking place
at a remote location in
the Middle East. You will
see it all: the nails
hit home, and then
the man himself
hoist high – witness
the pain as pinioned
hands and feet take up
the strain of body's
sagging weight."

Did you feel the
nails driven through
your hands, *your* feet:
experience,
not only the
shattering pain,
but the chattering
crowds, enjoying an
afternoon out, watching
you die – not in a
hospital bed, but
strung up on high?

Seen thus, and
experienced so –
albeit in mind's eye
and at imagination's
behest – could we
any longer ignore
the import of such
news, left undisturbed
on the printed page,
and sanitized by the
passage of full
two thousand
years?

Painswick Church
(A Soliloquy at the start of the Afghan War, 2001)

With darkness all about us,
the spire points heavenward still,
and clock, bright-lit, confronts us
with time present (with which,
'tis said, no other time compares).

Atop the spire the golden cock
keeps lonely watch on what
awaits the world below, by way of
wind and weather, and –
who knows what –
elsewise?

And we?
We flounder
on the ground, and –
at our peril – spurn the
heavenwards pointer, and
ignore the bright-lit reminder
that time present, flying fast,
becomes, irretrievably, time past,
its opportunities for ever lost;
and – in the darkness – oblivious
of the crossroads at our feet:

to left the old, tired, unwise,
worn-out ways; to right, a new
way, a new vision, which
points us to the skies.

'Peace' – and Peace

There is a peace, 'tis said, that
"passeth all understanding" –
words conjuring up an image
of the end of all strife,
all pain, all sorrow and
all fear;
       but the peace
outstripping human
apprehension surely
not that which comes
with the *end* of all
such, but is yet in
their very presence
known.

Perchance...

Often, do I wonder
what it will be like
to die – to be snuffed out
(as some would have it)
like a candle, or to
experience the ultimate
in metamorphoses.

  Is a butterfly
  able to remember
  what it was like to be
  a caterpillar, and so
  suffer the equivalent
  of culture shock? –
  the saving grace
  the time it spends
  as chrysalis.

Is death, then,
our chrysalis state –
which spares us
metamorphosing
in a trice from the
caterpillar crawl
of life on Earth
to the winged life
of the Spirit?

  'Perchance'
  (as it would seem)
  'to dream', but,
  could it be that,
  outside of time –
  slowly, and as
  imperceptibly as
  dawn turns into day –
  we wake up to the
  truth that it is, in fact,
  no dream at all, but
  the Eternity that
  Love needs,
  to tell it all
  in full?

Perfection in Love

Love looks not
for perfection
in the gift, or
in the giving,
and least of all
the giver – save only that
such imperfections
should not lie in
some ulterior motive,
or counting of the cost.

As for the love – of which
the gift itself is emblem –
it must be love of
"warts and all", or
no love at all the love
that it avows.

Prayer Before Breakfast

Take my life-long hope,
ambition, and desire to
follow You in all things,
great or small, and
turn them into reality,
even as You turned
the water into wine.

Open the doors of
my awareness to Your
indwelling presence:
of my life as part of
Your being; the source of
my strength and of my
inheritance – the peace "that
passeth all understanding."

With arms spread wide
and upward, to embrace
what- and *when*-ever,
I am – as best I can –
saying "Yes,"
"Yes," and
"YES!"
over,
and
again,
to Your gift
of life for this,
another
day.

Prayer in Need
is
Prayer Indeed

Lord,
I was on my
knees – no – not in
worship, but in
weakness: perhaps I
was even on all-fours.

But – you heard my
call, and helped me
to my feet again –
and I was able to
resume my daily
walk with
you.

For those unfamiliar with the Quaker way of worship, it needs to be pointed out that it is 'un-programmed', and based on silence, which should be broken only when one feels deeply moved enough to speak what are felt to be *worshipful* words. Quakers are no more perfect than their fellow humans, however! – and sometimes find themselves on their feet speaking words which would have been better left to speak over coffee – afterwards...

Quaker Meeting

'Hush thy mouth,'
the catch phrase went –
no Quaker, he, who coined it,
yet, could it be for us,
foregathered here,
the very word of God?

No slick rejoinder this – that we
the spoken word eschew; rather
is it laid upon us to speak the
words of ministry with 'hush' –
for speak we not
of God?

And, if 'hushed' words alone
be spoke, how many words –
too ready spoke – *un*-spoke
would be?

Questions...

'What does being religious mean?'
she asked, ingenuously.
'You see – I don't go to church,
but I do talk to him a lot –
I mean God,' she added, shyly.
'D'you think he listens?'

'I'm sure he does.'

'I don't mean just the big things –
you know – like when somebody dies.
I mean the little things as well,
like a bill I've been dreading
coming through the door,
and it's not nearly as much
as I'd thought it'd be –
I just say, "Thank you, God."
D'you think that's odd of me?'

'Not a bit. You see –
we all need someone to
thank, and not just to
ask for things. And
who better to thank,
than God?'

Recollections of Portmadoc

Such beauty lay outstretched for our embrace! –
of rolling earth, and splashing seas, and sky;
of creatures, too, that run, and swim, and fly,
each in its element, its own true place;
of bracken's flaming gold, and rainbow's trace,
of lush green meadow's sun-splashed patchwork shape,
and diamond snow-cap set 'gainst sky's drab drape;
of heaven mirrored in the lake's calm face.

We stood beneath the spell of mountain stream,
of lap at water's edge, and curlew's call,
to watch the sun's rise glint and gleam
on sea's soft swell, and fleck cascading fall.
And as we looked, and listened, did it seem,
the beauty we embraced, embraced us all.

Sea-change

Washed up, on a
strange and hostile
shore, long had I
languished,
high and dry –
far from the sea,
and its endless,
ever-beckoning,
activity.

Then –
'Get your feet wet again,'
said a still small voice
within. 'I'll see you back
down the stony beach,
as far as the water's edge.
It will be up to you then, to
take the plunge.'

Buoyed up by
the salty water,
refreshed by its
tangy taste, I
struck out for the
deep once more,
immersed in life
again.

Spirit's Husbandry

To cultivate quietness
at day's beginning is, as well,
to sow its seeds in the virgin soil
of hours yet to come, where,
as day progresses, they will
germinate, sending forth
tall stems and broad leaves,
until, in due time, the fruits
appear – ripening when the
heat of day is at its height;
their cooling juices ready
and waiting then, to quench
spirit's mounting thirst, in an
oasis of peace, created by
the lush green foliage.

Take a Breath

'Enjoy your day,'
she said, as
I paid my bill, and
went on my way —
my load the lighter
for her words;
just three of them,
conveyed on a single,
out-going breath,
to leave me pondering:
how many times have we
wasted our breath,
not when words
have been unheeded,
but have gone
unspoken?

Telephone

It rests snugly
in the palm −
like a baby
on its mother's
arm, and is described
as "cordless", which
means there's no
visible umbilical,
connecting it
to base.
And its memory
is prodigious! −
knowing, instantly,
just who it is
who's trying to
ring me up.

   In fact, come to
   think of it, it's
   quite like me
   in a way,
   having − in the
   absence of that
   visible umbilical −
   an *in*-visible means
   of communicating
   with headquarters,
   which is instantaneous,
   and unimpeded, even
   by the infinitudes
   of space.

But, sad to say,
how often I fail to
recognize who it is that's
trying to get through to me −

despite the fact that
it might be
God.

The Birthday Card

This blank card
no assistance gives
to me, whose need
just now, above all else,
is words.

Why then should I have made
difficult more difficult,
by discarding printed
"messages", offered
for pence, to express
the inexpressible?
The reason, indeed,
just that – but no card
honest enough
to say so, or it
might have made a
sale for the lady who,
far side of the counter,
strove so enthusiastically
to solve the insoluble
with, 'This is a pretty one',
or, 'Does she appreciate
humour?' (A "funny" one, this,
with large, rough, red tongue
protruding, ostensibly to
make you laugh,
where love, in its
fullness, brings
welling tears –
and silence.)

And silence, written down, is
but a blank page, dearest one;
and so, blank page it was
I purchased, to express as
honestly as could be,
the joy – inexpressible –
of your love for me,
so undeserved, and
my poor, halting love
for thee.

But though this "silence"
best express my love
in simple tenderness,
where words leave off,
these beauteous blooms
can start to have their say.

Look then upon these flowers
and see reflected there,
in truest beauty,
thy dear self.

(May 23rd 1960)

The Catalyst

Contemplation –
the laboratory
of the Spirit:
where things
begin to happen
when, in seemingly
doing nothing,
we do all.

Thoughts effervesce,
ideas crystallize;
moods change colour,
hard feelings evaporate
into thin air, and the
bare bones of intuition
receive their flesh. And –
yes, indeed – all this
by seemingly
doing nothing,
nothing at all:
contemplation
the all-enabling
catalyst.

But – truth is –
it goes against the
grain, does it not? I mean –
things don't just
happen.

Yet that
is exactly
what they seem
to do when God is
Prime Mover, and
Sole Cause.

Another poem written in the aftermath of my wife's first stroke in 1968.

The Emmaus Road

Lord, be with me,
walk with me in the way,
towards a new Emmaus,
at the end of day.
Then come Thou in
and sup with me,
open Thou mine eyes,
to see in the bread
that brokenness
must needs forerun
a rising from the dead.
So, teach Thou me
die to the past,
in present brokenness,
that this essential
yester-death may yield
a morrow resurrection.

The Question Is...

"God is love – and he that
dwelleth in love dwelleth in
God, and God in him."

A mere theological postulate,
with which we are all too
familiar, and long since *passé?* –
or the very *raison d'être* of the
quarks and leptons, and
all the rest, that make up
our Universe? –

and us.

The Question to End all Questions –
and Answers

The news was full of it.

'*Why,* **Why, WHY?'** -
the words erupting from my lips
like a burst water main, and as
unstemmable. Strangely, he didn't
seem offended: in fact, he said he'd
been expecting it. But, the last thing
I was expecting was his answer.

'They pinioned me with iron nails
to a wooden cross, and lifted me up
to die,' he said. 'That was *my*
Rottweiler experience. And, yes,
it happens all over again, whenever
a child gets mauled to death by
a dog, or grown-ups tortured and
killed, by men;

'when tectonic plates collide, and
tornados and tsunami waves
bring sudden death to thousands;
when pandemics sweep from
continent to continent like
storm-force winds, cutting
a swathe of death through
whole populations; when men
yield to hatred and wage
unholy war – I am there,
to share their agony.

'And, when the dreaded diagnosis
rings in your ears, it rings in my ears
too; when life is slipping away, I am
there, to die, anew, with you.
Creator of all that is,
from the Milky Way, to the
meanest flower that blows; and,
suffering all – from the
collision of whole galaxies,
to the death of a little child –
my strength is yet in
weakness, and
my power
in love.'

The Tyranny of Time

Was it
to the knowledge of
time that Eve betrayed us,
and through that knowledge,
down the ages, placed Man
in thrall to its tyranny?

  Insidiously does the
  knowledge present itself:
  as an awareness of a
  past, lost irretrievably, a
  present, grasped feverishly,
  a future, faced fearfully – with
  death its consummation.

On this,
time's treadmill,
there appeared
a Man, who said,
'I am come that
they might have life,
and have it more
abundantly.'
"Life everlasting,"
it came to be called –
conjuring up images
of an endless span
of days becoming
yesterdays, and
morrows waiting
to become today.
Little wonder that
men, too long tied
to time's tyranny,
turn empty, away.

  Truth is, though, that
  the life He came
  to give is lived in
  the Eternal Now –
  where the past
  is ever redeemable,
  the future emancipate
  from fear, and the
  present moment set,
  like a precious jewel,
  in the gold clasp
  of Eternity –
  to redeem us,
  at long last, from
  the tyranny
  of time.

Thoughts, post-Christmas

"Unto us a child is born" –
parenthood, it's called,
but, terms and conditions
apply; although, these days,
it must be said, the small print
too often goes unread.

    Be that as it may,
    yet doubt not that
    the small print is
    getting bigger and
    bolder by the day –
    no longer possible
    to ignore, or for
    parenthood to be
    restricted to fulfilling
    the dictates of
    the Selfish Gene.

All too well now,
do we know
that safeguarding
our offspring is
no longer to safeguard
the future of *their*
offspring, and *their*
offspring's offspring
from the consequences
of a lifestyle that
threatens survival,
generations on.

    Make no mistake: we,
    the present bearers of
    an All-Too-Selfish Gene,
    needs must undergo a
    sea-change in the way we
    live, if the children of
    our children's children
    are, in fact, to
    live at all.

Time

'Words fail me,'
as they say – of actions,
circumstances, or
events exceeding
the bounds of human
decency, endurance,
or belief.

Words fail the
moment, not the
man, and need the
catalyst of time, which –
like an enzyme, working
for the emotions – enables
heart, mind, and spirit to
assimilate what would be
impossible to swallow
in the instant, whole.
Thus – ingested – can the
most unpalatable of
happenings provide the
fruits of wisdom for
the biding soul.

**To Care, or not to Care ,
That is the Question**

We can live
without care
for man or beast –
care-less even in our
treatment of the least
of God's own creatures.

Yet might we still live
free of care (though far from
care-*less*), in a state – yes! –
of *holy carefree-ness* –

but full of
holy care.

Top-Up

You see, this vehicle,
I was given it, for life,
so I need to make
regular visits to the
filling station, for a
top-up. There – with
fuel cap removed,
and supply line in place –
the fuel flows freely
into my depleted tank.

    In it goes – a rich mix
    of love distilled, and
    unadulterated joy, of
    peace unalloyed, and
    strength according to
    my need – the fuel gauge
    indicating then, that
    my vehicle is once more
    fit and ready
    for the road.

To cap it all
(as might be said),
the pump flags up
"No Charge for this
Replenishment", and –
what is more – in place of
a receipt – it issues a
printed sheet, guaranteeing
that all components of
the fuel supplied are
heart-, not global-
warming.

Truth – *Embodied*

George Fox spoke of
'that of God in
everyone', but,
yet larger truth is
'that of everyone
in God': Christ
the vine, and
each of us
a branch thereof,
according to
Saint John; or,
as Paul has it,
'We, being many,
are one body
in Christ.'

   Too familiar
   by far, are we, with
   such soul-shaking
   affirmations, which,
   taken seriously,
   would, for ever,
   change our lives.
   But – alas – we
   pass them by
   like familiar faces
   in the street,
   to whom a nod of
   recognition is
   deemed adequate
   acknowledgement of
   their embodied
   truth.

In such manner
does the greatest
of all truths
escape us: that
God is neither
simply "out there".
nor is he just
"a God within",
but, truly, are *we*
in, and of,
his very Being;
and in whom
thus resides our
true identity.

Tsunami

It was as if,
mere moments
before, I had been
the sole occupant
of a deserted beach,
to be overwhelmed,
mere moments after,
by a veritable tsunami
of fresh insight and
awareness – of
what was, and
what was not:
that the beach – far from
deserted – was,
in truth, deep within
my very self, and
that, moreover,
I was not alone:
the real "scandal of
particularity" *not* that
it all began with a
singular "Big Bang",
but that the
Creator of all,
from the galaxy-
great, to the subatomic-
small, should choose
me (and you) for
his place to
Be.

Two Crosses

Gold had pierced
her ears – gently,
anaesthetically, (and
antiseptically, of course) –
pendent, from each,
a gold cross.
Fine pair of ornaments
they were, and
at what cost to her,
in cash?

    Iron had pierced His hands –
    and feet – savagely:
    pain-packed pinions
    driven, hate-poisoned,
    into a rough-hewn
    wooden cross, and
    at what cost to Him,
    in pain?

And as, on either side of her,
so, each side of Him,
a cross –
but of wood,
not gold –

and on each,
a dying man.

'Up' — or 'Down'?

What happened
to the Present Moment —
the Eternal Now, where
dwells the Child, and
over which not even
Einstein has any
jurisdiction:
where time stands still,
today refuses to
become yesterday,
and tomorrow
never comes?

They *say* we "grow up" —
but might it be that
in some ways we
"grow down",
instead?

Vesper

Gently the day gives way to the night,
slowly the sun withdraws its light,
quietly, the Spirit, casting its spell,
God's benediction, 'All shall be well.'

Swiftly the stars outspread the sky,
brightly the moon sheds her light on high –
light of the Spirit, casting its spell,
God's benediction, 'All shall be well.'

Lightly, the night breeze blows through the tree,
softly, its whisper speaks to me –
voice of the Spirit, casting its spell,
God's benediction, 'All shall be well.'

("Vesper" was set to music for four-part choir in 2004.)

This poem's style is deliberately colloquial - *and* hard-hitting...

When A Prayer
Is Not *Prayer*

'Heal the sick, strengthen
the weak in mind or spirit,
comfort the bereaved, be
company for the lonely, and
enfold in your love all who
suffer for your sake.'

   'What's that?' you say.
   Believe it (or not), it's a prayer –
   to be heard from almost any pulpit
   on a Sunday, or any day
   "over the air".

But, in truth,
is it not rather a
Job Description for the
Deity, or a Work Sheet for
his day? And, in all honesty
(and not to put too fine a
point on it) isn't it really
the equivalent of teaching
grandma to suck eggs?

   So you're shocked by
   such comparison of the
   sublime with the near-
   ridiculous? Then think how
   shocked dear God must be, so
   earnestly requested to do those
   very things he's been doing since
   human life began – and, what's more,
   asked in a manner that suggests
   that he might otherwise have
   fallen down on the job.

And there's worse to come,
the request seemingly implying
that, in making it, we had fulfilled
our task, discharged our duty,
when, in fact, we had done
nothing, nothing at all –
other than to cross out
our names on the envelope,
and write "Return to Sender".

When Darkness is Light

'I form the light,
and create darkness' –
God's words, according to
the prophet – the implication:
that we must first experience
light, to know what
darkness is, a fact
so obvious as to
border on the trite,
but for the prime part
assigned by God
to night.

For, it is in darkness
that he reveals himself
most plainly: to the soul
no longer preoccupied with
his gifts, that, in the light, were,
for so long, for God himself
mistaken.

Thus does the
God of Paradox
exemplify how strange
is Truth – that the
greatest illumination
comes in soul's
Darkest Night.

When the Answer Came
Before the Question

In my life there is a
garden which, day upon day
(and often before first light),
I visit; there's no-one else
about. Or so I thought,
until – one morning – there,
in the shadows, was a
figure whom I (as did
another) might well have
mistaken for the
gardener, asking him
the question that was
ever on my lips.

But, *he* spoke first: just my
name – that was all. But
he had given me the
answer I had sought
lifelong. It was the
way he said it:
I simply *knew*
that it was
He.

IN MEMORY
OF
MARY AND ROGER

FOR MARY

You saw me first tonight,
and waved! – and
made a space for me,
a place for me, beside you,
on the bed.

Right from the start
we talked –
oh, how we talked! –
you plainly,
so plainly, at first;
and after,
in that little burble
interspersed
with laughter;
for tonight what matter that
meanings sometimes went astray
in wordless chatter?

What matter?
we met! –
oh, how we met! –
in a fourth dimension,
not of Einstein's time,
but freed
of its constraint
and tension –
where future
had no past,
and past no future;
and the present moment,
fleeting no longer,
became
the Eternal Now –
the place of
all true meeting.

(An early hospital visit, following Mary's first stroke)

Slow steps
on familiar ground,
with carpet's edge
a dangerous ledge,
and single stair
a precipice,
fraught
with grave peril.
The mountaineer
in all his strength,
roped
to stalwart colleagues,
with the blue sky
and the towering peaks
above
to challenge him,
knows nothing
of your sort of courage;
his risk
seems small,
and his objective
near,
compared with yours,
a few feet away;
as,
scorning help,
with walking frame
and calliper
you move,
step by step,
precariously,
alone in your weakness,
towards
the fireside chair.

The year wears on –
the magic mists appear,
casting their immemorial spell;
and leaves, fresh green
when you were well,
are turning brown, then red,
and, twisting in the chill wind, fall
as dead – shed
like sad confetti.

Daily, the artist sun,
with prodigal palette,
paints cosmic canvases;
and, night by night,
the stark stars,
piercing the canopy of evening,
stave off, still,
the gathering dark.

And birds, on branch and eave,
incredulously yet sing,
to catch my spirit
off-guard,
and evoke
the fierce pang
of remembered joy –
joy that I scarce now
dare contemplate.

Too easy it was,
by far,
to take you for granted
when you were well:
all too easy
to be preoccupied
with trivia –
to open the door
and peck you with a kiss
and say,
straightway,
'Do you know
what so-and-so did
today?'
Too easy
to but half-listen,
and never to stop
and wonder
at the music of your voice;
to let pass,
unsung,
your grace of movement,
the marvellous coordination
of foot with foot,
that we call
"walking" –
too easy,
all too easy,
so.

markably, several months after Mary's first stroke, we were able to take a brief holiday at the Worm's Head Hotel, South Wales. The sight of the festive place-settings in the dining room prompted this poem. The reference is to an Elizabethan restaurant in Guildford, where, earlier in the year, we had celebrated Mary's birthday.

Menus on the tables,
places neatly laid —
sparkling glasses
waiting to be filled —
chairs disposed
invitingly;
and, over all,
the soft light
of the table lamps,
casting their benedictory air.

And I thought of the time —
oh, so little time ago! —
when I took you out to dine;
we sat in the sixteenth-century bay,
overhanging the busy street,
as, Elizabethan-gay,
we laughed,
and ate,
and studied the passers-by.
And the toast was "To us!"
as we raised the wine,
and your right hand held the glass —
oh, God —
your right hand held the glass.

Pull up the chairs!
Poke up the fire!
And curl up cosily! –
for this week's
Colour Supplement
invites us
to choose
where we might go –
to escape
the winter
within.

And let the chatter
be loud enough
that the sound
of the moan
in the wind
may be drowned.

Turn on the light!
Draw curtains tight!
(Yes! turn on
sweet music, too) –
and we'll play a game
of make-believe
that there *is* no darkness
outside:
better to bask in
fluorescent tube's light
than risk
an encounter
with God
in the night.

'Bloody bad luck,'
he said,
as he drove from the fifteenth tee,
but it was not of his drive
that he spoke,
but of me.
(His ball went into the rough.)

'Yes –
his wife –
it happened in June,
and we've hardly seen him since;
they despaired of her life
at the time –
even now she can't be left.'
(They searched for the little white ball,
that, of course, was all in all –
"three off the tee"
it would otherwise be.)
'Damned bad luck –
just think,
he's probably washing up!'
(I was.)
'Poor bloody bod,
perhaps
he's even
praying to God.'
(That also was true.)

They found the ball
(and another one, too),
and he chopped it out
with his Nine.
'We might save the hole,'
(his partner said)
'if the next one
finds the green –
yes, it's damned bad luck
when a chap has to chuck
his golf.'

By the time they had reached
the Nineteenth,
the washing-up was done,
and my belov'd was up and dressed,
and settled in her chair,
and had started to practise
to write her name
with a hand that still rebelled,
as they downed their beers,
and swallowed their fears
that life might not be
always
a game.

Early morning
gives no warning
of a sunset
less than eternity away:
no need to plan the day.

Mid-morning
is refreshment time –
let's take a breather
from our play
(the sunshine has surely come to stay).

High noon,
and native powers
intoxicate
with the sense
that the choice is ours:
there is nothing we could not do
if we wanted to –
but we don't.

By afternoon
the shadow
of a doubt
appears:
the sun seems not quite so high
(could it be that it threatens
to set –
and that in a finite time?).

Late afternoon,
and a nip in the air –
better to have a care –
there is no doubt now
that the night exists,
and the light is getting low.

But – could it be
that sun's dying glow
yet symbols
a promise,
born of diminishment
and fulfilled
at day's end?

The world goes by:
young lovers kiss
in the streets,
and ageing couples
saunter,
scanning the windows
for bargains
in tomorrow's sales.
Old people sit,
slightly apart,
on the seats;
and young bloods
thunder past
astride their machines,
thirsting for trouble –
oblivious, all,
of the miracle
of arms
and legs,
and simple conversation.

Now you are coming home,
my love —
home to us all!
Yet, were truth better served
to say that home
is coming back to us —
for you *are* home!
Bricks and mortar
have ever been
merely the place
for you to be
what you are:
wife,
mother,
friend of all!
So —
Sing bricks!
Sing mortar!
And sing, my darling daughter!
Rejoice, my sons! —
for home is coming back
to each and all
of us.

Not to get used
to the sound of your foot
dragging reluctantly
across the floor
behind your walking frame,
which you manoeuvre
like an unwilling mule
you are desperately trying
to tame;

   not to get used
   to the sight of your face,
   frustration-fraught,
   as you strive for the word
   that is pikestaff-plain
   to your inner eye,
   but you struggle to say,
   in vain;

not to get used
to the clutch of your hand
on my arm
as we dare the two steps
to the garden below –
a journey whose hazards
you, only, can know;

   not to get used
   to the thought
   that once was a time
   when foot followed foot
   in so graceful
   a walk,
   and word followed word
   in a torrent
   of talk,
   and arm tucked in arm
   just for love
   not support;

God! –
not to get used
to these things,
I say,
not to get used to them, God,
I pray.

Let me
at least take comfort
from my tears –
that there is yet left
enough of me
to weep,
not simply, now, for loss of you,
but for a myriad
unacknowledged pains,
deep buried
by the wayside
of our journey
through those stricken years.

   'I weep,
   therefore I am' –
   thus do I reassure myself
   that desolation
   has not laid final waste
   to me;
   yet
   on that journey
   did I, like those
   in heat of battle smitten,
   soldier on,
   unaware
   that when the strife was at an end
   I would have mortal wounds
   to tend.

Weep then,
scan the bleak landscape
of those fraught, fateful years,
drink the full draught
of unassimilated pain,
and the then un-shed,
countless tears.

---------- **Bereavement** ----------

Many said
that it was over now;
others, that I should be thankful;
a few (I fear) that it was simply
God's will that had been done
(like the hurricane last year…) –
but I knew the life, which,
in my heart,
had only just begun.

Death gave it birth: your passing
the cosmic contraction
that propelled me
on the head-first journey
through the tortuous tunnel
of fierce disbelief,
with pain beyond thought,
into a future
furnished
with an empty chair,
an empty bed,
coats still hanging, ready,
in the hall;
your place at table vacant,
meal on meal.

Morning upon morning,
listless and leaden-eyed
I lie,
hoping the world
will pass me by.
What chance of that? –
the harsh light of reality
leaves no margin
for the re-interpretation
of events;
better to weep my way
into the crevices
of yet another day –
others, perchance,
will neither find
nor even seek me
there.

But –
tread warily;
at every twist and turn
of time
and space
there lies in wait
some devastating evocation
of the past,
beyond tears –
from a paper scrap,
with frail words
traced by that rebellious hand,
to your first calliper, lurking
in the dark depths
of a wardrobe
where I sought
a long-lost pair of shoes.
(God alone knows
the volumes spoken
by a piece of bent iron
fitted with a leather thong
and metal peg –
the vision, too,
that it evoked
of you,
with your strapped leg
and walking frame,
and those first faltering steps –
God, indeed, alone knows
the courage that you showed.)

Beyond tears, yes,
but weep noneless;
grief's work
will not be done,
till grief itself
dies, in childbirth –
its progeny hope's glimmer,
lighting the darkest recess
of my breaking heart.

Each day
a lifetime:

  each waking
  a birth,
  with its fierce pang
  for the lost womb
  of the night,
  its first breath
  deep-drawn in protest
  at the burgeoning of day;

each morning
a childhood,
deprived
of its innocent obliviousness
of Man's mortality;

  high noon
  a middle age
  of unfulfilled intentions
  failing to survive
  the close scrutiny
  of day;

each afternoon
a retirement, forfeit
to a frantic foraging
for the mislaid meaning
of the past, and hope
with which to face
a boding future;

  each evening
  an old age
  graced,
  surprisingly enough,
  by a brief acceptance
  of things as they are;
  and night
  a return
  to the darkness
  of unknowing.

FOR ROGER

The very first poem of the eleven that follow was written down, almost in a stupor, within a few hours of learning of the sudden death of my beloved son, Roger - architect, and painter. The next two or three were written in a matter of days, following this tragic event, and the remainder within just a few weeks more.

09 – 02 - 05

A huge hunk of me died today.
I didn't have any say
in the matter –
it happened,
just like that.
I've still got
two arms,
two legs,
two ears,
two eyes,
a nose that
still smells,
and a tongue that
still tastes,
but I am less
one son,
I am less
one son –
I am less,
I am less,
I am *less*...

'Thank you for coming,' I said,
the last time he called –
I always did.
And I always shall –
'Thank you for coming,'
'Thank you for coming,'
'Thank you for coming,'...

I rang him
to find out
what his day
had been like.
'Dad,' he said,
'can I ring you back?'
'Of course,' I said,
And I'm sure he will,
I'm *sure* he will…

He never seemed absent-minded –
except, that is,
when he was eating biscuits.
Then, his hand would
steal towards the packet –
even whilst he was talking,
and, seemingly, of its own accord.

But – and here's a strange thing –
it always seemed to know
when it'd reached
the last one in the packet,
politely, then, desisting.

And – redolent of him
beyond all words –
I've just come upon
the *last* last one.
It was a Custard Cream.

Thick, and heavy,
the pigments,
as he applied them
to the canvas,
adding a third dimension,
and, along with it, a fourth –
not time-wise,
but eternal –
as he replaced
the drab colours
of a still life
with vibrant choices
of his own.
And the lifeless still
would begin to dance
with life,
until – as he worked on –
he was satisfied
that its message
would be plain
for all to see:
that joy,
for him,
was, indeed, a richly,
many-coloured thing.

His pen and ink drawings
were as delicate
as his paintings were robust:
the paintings almost without exception
of still life subjects, the drawings
of buildings, streets, and interiors,
and mainly of his beloved, rural France –
Saurat, Noula, and Ruvenac –
whole sets of them hanging,
in columns, on the wall,
and – far from competing –
each one
a foil
to all the rest.

But perhaps the one I remember
and loved the best,
was Four, St Mary's Buildings,
from across the road, at night –
presided over
by a crescent moon –
his Christmas card,
some years ago

Number Four,
St. Mary's Buildings, had a
paved courtyard at the back,
with a high wall and a
close-boarded door,
hiding the view of a
grassy bank and
flowering shrubs,
wild flowers –
and more.

But Roger had other plans.
'Let's go for a little ride.'
And off we went, on a
mystery tour, to the most
unlikely place
ever to grace
the countryside –
what might have been
a field of wheat
stacked high and wide
with enough of this, that, and
the other to build a whole street,
and more, much more –
a "reclamation yard":
grey tiles of stone and slate –
warm brown, of terra-cotta –
bricks, multi-hued,
kilned centuries before,
and paving slabs galore;
a bevy of garden figurines
in deep discourse with
one another,
whilst a host of disoriented
sundials hotly disputed
the time of day.
And there was more,
much more.

How Roger loved to browse! –
enthusing over a Victorian
marble wash-stand with its
ornate, and generously
proportioned
bowl – or the sheer
grotesqueness
of a gargoyle, hand-carved, in
stone.

But, enough! –
he came to the point at last:
we were actually seeking
a wrought-iron gate
to replace that wooden door
and open up the view.

He got as near to sneering
as he was ever likely to –
at some modern, twirly,
factory-produced horrors
(as he regarded them),
until, at last, we came upon
what he had sought so avidly:
a simple, yet so elegant,
hand-made specimen – as old,
maybe, as Number Four.

To me, it seemed
almost as plain
as plain could be,
but Roger could already
see what was denied to me –
a Regency-crafted gate
at home at last in the
gap between two
Georgian stone walls.
and difficult, indeed, to tell
which the more beautiful –
the gate, or the
view through:

Roger, the jeweller,
had found,
for his gem,
its true, and
rightful setting.

It was the nearest to boasting
that I ever heard him get.
'Actually, there's nothing to it, Dad.
I just tell her* about the cash
that's failed to come in,
and the cash
we expect to arrive
within a month
(or maybe two),
and she simply says,
'That's fine.' '

But,
in all innocence,
he'd left out
the most important fact
of all:
it was his total guilelessness,
that she was banking on.

*The lady referred to was a manageress at the bank handling Roger's firm's business.

How eagerly
he contemplated
retirement,
just a year away! –
hoarding brushes,
paints,
and canvases
against the day
when he would once more
have time,
space,
and opportunity to paint
to his heart's content
again.

And how sadly
we mourned,
on his behalf,
that lost opportunity! –
and, on our own account,
the paintings that we,
now, would never see.

How suddenly, then,
did I realize that this
was not a moment
to mourn the loss
of the paintings
that would never be!–
or, for that matter,
the buildings that
he would have added
to his name,
monumentally.

Rather was it
the moment
to celebrate
all those paintings
that he *did* leave for us
to contemplate –
and the buildings
that will stand for
decades to come:
paintings and buildings, all,
witness to the freshness
of his vision,
and his quiet –
so special –
joie de vivre.

There were many sides
to Roger:
the architect, of course,
his buildings ever and always
breathing freshness
and new life – the "Roger" touch;
the painter, too,
each painting
a successive chapter
of his quest
for his particular
holy grail –
the secrets of the Universe
embodied in the language
of colour, juxtaposed.

But that's just a beginning:
in the most unobtrusive way
imaginable
he lived, and loved
unsparingly –
as husband,
son,
brother,
and son-in-law;
as father,
and, latterly –
and oh, so proud! –
grandfather.
Yet, vying
with this rich tapestry
of family life
was the backdrop
to all life as he saw it –
a fabric of friendship
so warm, so rare,
offered to all and sundry
without a single thought or
care that life should, or could,
be otherwise.

And the evidence for that? –
the world and his wife
that came to say
'Thank you,' at
his funeral.

Let there no misunderstanding be:
had he, in truth, received a knighthood
for his architecture,
or even been raised to the peerage
in recognition of his work,
and,
furthermore,
had become an Academician
for his painting –
had any,
or all,
of these
come to pass,
they would have counted for
little by comparison with
his accomplishments
in the arts of living,
loving, sharing, and
caring for all the little,
precious things that
make up this human life.

Would all those who turned up
at his funeral have come
simply to celebrate the fact
that he was Lord Roger,
or even Academician Kemp?
No! –
peers are ten a penny,
academicians three for the
price of two.
But Roger?

There was just *one*
of him.

THE CURRENCY OF LOVE

Love has a currency
all its own:

its smallest denomination
is of inestimable worth –
yet it is thief-proof,
and needs no protection.

Minted freely,
It creates no fear of inflation –
in fact, it reverses all the usual rules.

Thus, unless it is counterfeit,
its investment seeks no return;
and income actually increases
with expenditure.

Its nature is always to be
a gift:
it cannot therefore be earned,
or claimed as any kind of recompense
or reward;
and, when returned,
it needs to be immediately
re-invested,
for the attempt to hoard it
leads to bankruptcy.

It defies drawing up a balance sheet,
for it cannot be enumerated;
and any attempt to put a price on it
renders it worthless.

It is always available on demand,
and requires no security;
indeed,
it may take the form
of a blank cheque,
with the consequences
willingly accepted –
for counting the cost
is foreign to it.

It is exchangeable
the world over,
but such exchange
must always be
person to person:
no broker
can have dealings in it
to achieve a cheap gain.

It can be taxed
to the limit,
yet emerge
with enhanced reserves.

It is the only currency
adequate to meet the cost
of living.

THE LAST WORD

Let the cosmologist predict
what he has to, of the future
of us humans: of Planet Earth,
and our local star we call the Sun –
destined, in several billion years,
to become a Red Giant, capable of
gobbling up the Earth for
breakfast, or toasting it
for tea.

What matters it to love? –
love which, in life's Nowness
is yet experienced in a
fourth dimension – not of
Einstein's time, but of
Eternity: love which has been
Evolution's goal since
time began, and will
outlive even an
overcooked
and obese
Sun.